BOXING DOMINATION

WIN EVERY FIGHT!

A 21-Day Program to Psych-Out, Confuse, Frustrate, and Beat Your Opponent in Boxing and Mixed Martial Arts

SAMMY FRANCO

Also by Sammy Franco

Power Boxing Workout Secrets
Speed Boxing Secrets
Heavy Bag Training
Heavy Bag Combinations
Heavy Bag Workout
The Heavy Bag Bible
Double End Bag Training
The Complete Body Opponent Bag Book
Cane Fighting
The Widow Maker Compendium
Invincible: Mental Toughness Techniques for Peak Performance
Unleash Hell: A Step-by-Step Guide to Devastating Widow Maker Combinations
Feral Fighting: Advanced Widow Maker Fighting Techniques
The Widow Maker Program: Extreme Self-Defense for Deadly Force Situations
Savage Street Fighting: Tactical Savagery as a Last Resort
Stand and Deliver: A Street Warrior's Guide to Tactical Combat Stances
Maximum Damage: Hidden Secrets Behind Brutal Fighting Combinations
First Strike: End a Fight in Ten Seconds or Less!
The Bigger They Are, The Harder They Fall
Self-Defense Tips and Tricks
Kubotan Power: Quick & Simple Steps to Mastering the Kubotan Keychain
Gun Safety: For Home Defense and Concealed Carry
Out of the Cage: A Guide to Beating a Mixed Martial Artist on the Street
Warrior Wisdom: Inspiring Ideas from the World's Greatest Warriors
War Machine
1001 Street Fighting Secrets
When Seconds Count: Self-Defense for the Real World
Killer Instinct: Unarmed Combat for Street Survival
Street Lethal: Unarmed Urban Combat

Boxing Domination
Copyright © 2018 by Sammy Franco
ISBN: 978-1-941845-60-8
Printed in the United States of America

Published by Contemporary Fighting Arts, LLC.
Visit us Online at: **SammyFranco.com**

All rights reserved. Except for use in a review, no portion of this book may be reproduced in any form without the express written permission of the author. Direct inquiries and/or orders to the above address.

For author interviews or publicity information, please send inquiries in care of the publisher.

Contents

About Boxing Domination — VII

Boxing Styles and Techniques — 1

Chapter 1: Bait and Smash — 21

Chapter 2: The Roundabout — 31

Chapter 3: Cover and Crush — 37

Chapter 4: The Steamroller — 45

Chapter 5: Catch Me Now — 53

Chapter 6: Boxing Domination Exercises — 65

Chapter 7: Boxing Domination Workout Programs — 79

Glossary — 97

About Sammy Franco — 127

"It is not difficult to be unconventional in the eyes of the world when your unconventionality is but the convention of your set."

–W. Somerset Maugham

Disclaimer!

The author, publisher, and distributors of this book disclaim any liability from loss, injury, or damage, personal or otherwise, resulting from the information and procedures in this book. This book is for academic study only.

The information contained in this book is not designed to diagnose, treat, or manage any physical health conditions.

Before you begin any exercise or activity, including those suggested in this book, it is important to check with your physician to see if you have any condition that might be aggravated by strenuous training.

About Boxing Domination

Boxing Domination: A 21-Day Program to Psych-Out, Confuse, Frustrate, and Beat Your Opponent in Boxing and Mixed Martial Arts is a unique program made for fighters (both boxers and mixed martial artists) who want to dominate and ultimately beat their opponents in the ring. In fact, when used correctly, this one-of-a-kind boxing program will produce excellent results in as little as twenty-one days.

Boxing Domination is different from any other boxing training book. Actually, the "unconventional" boxing techniques, tactics and strategies featured in this book are seldom seen or discussed in boxing circles. Nevertheless, these unorthodox techniques will allow you to psych-out and quickly dominate your opponent in boxing, mixed martial arts, and kick boxing.

With lots of detailed photographs and easy-to-follow instructions, Boxing Domination has beginner, intermediate and advanced training programs that will dramatically enhance and expand your fighting repertoire.

Best of all, this unique boxing training program works seamlessly with you current boxing program or combat sports workout routine. The only prerequisite is an open mind and a willingness to apply the tactics and strategies discussed in this book.

All of the domination boxing techniques featured in this book are based on my 30+ years of research, training, and teaching the fighting arts and their related disciplines. In fact, I have taught these unique boxing techniques to my top students, and I'm confident they will help you achieve success in the ring.

Since this is both a skill-building workbook and training guide, feel free to write in the margins, underline passages, and dog-ear the pages.

Finally, I encourage you to read this book from beginning to end, chapter by chapter. Only after you have read the entire book should you treat it as a reference and skip around, reading those chapters that directly apply to your needs.

Train hard!

Sammy Franco

Boxing Styles and Techniques
Making Sense of It All

Boxing Domination

The "Sweet and Sour" Science of Boxing

Professional Boxing is often called the Sweet Science. In fact, it's one of the most paradoxical sports known to humankind. On the one hand, it's a violent, barbaric sport requiring each fighter to inflict as much physical damage to his opponent. While on the other side, it's a beautiful, physical art form displaying some of the greatest human attributes, including courage, emotional and physical resilience, determination, and athleticism.

To the trained eye, boxing is also a scientific sport, loaded with hidden nuances that requiring a tremendous amount of strategy and planning – similar to a game of chess. Except, in this game, you can get seriously injured.

Regardless of how you view boxing (loving or despising it), there's no denying that it's one of the most exciting sporting events. And, most importantly, it's a sport that is here to stay.

Foundational Boxing Skills

The success and failure of a boxer or mixed martial artist (professional or amateur) will largely depend on his or her foundational skills and attributes. This means they must learn and master the basics of the sport. Some of these foundational skills include:

- **Boxing Stance**
- **Boxing Footwork**
- **Boxing Techniques**
- **Boxing Attributes**

For those of you who are new to boxing, I will briefly cover these concepts, and for those of you with a solid boxing background, please feel free to move on to the next section titled *Boxing Styles*.

The Boxing Stance

Any coach worth his salt will agree that a boxer's ability to hit hard begins with his stance. The fighter must master a boxing stance that always places his feet, hips and shoulders in the proper position to deliver explosive blows. For a right handed fighter, this means the following:

- Left side of your body faces the opponent.
- Left foot extended forward approximately a shoulder width distance from the rear foot.
- Right foot pointing toward the opponent.
- 50% weight distribution on each leg.

Boxing Styles and Techniques: Making Sense of It All

- Knees are slightly bent.
- Torso is slightly bent.
- Both hands are up and close to your face.
- Front and rear elbows close to the body and pointing down.
- Shoulders are relaxed but ready.
- Eyes looking forward at the opponent with chin angled down.

Footwork

Footwork is an essential component of boxing because it determines your ability to move and strategically position yourself in the ring. However, many boxers don't realize that footwork also plays two important roles for delivering devastating knockout power.

Range Finder - Footwork facilitates finding your range, which permits you to reach your target at the ideal distance, which will maximize the impact power of your punch.

Power Amplifier - Footwork functions as a power amplifier for your fighting techniques. Body momentum generated from footwork also acts as a power generator for your punching skills.

Boxing footwork and mobility are one and the same. I define mobility as the ability to move your body quickly and freely, which is accomplished through basic footwork. The safest footwork involves quick, economical steps performed on the balls of your feet, while you remain relaxed and balanced. Keep in mind that balance is your most important consideration.

Basic boxing footwork can be used for both offensive and defensive purposes, and it is structured around four general directions: forward, backward, right, and left. However, always remember this footwork rule of thumb: Always move the foot closest

Boxing Domination

to the direction you want to go first, and let the other foot follow an equal distance. This will always keep the feet apart from each other and prevent cross-stepping, which can cost you the fight.

Basic Footwork Movements

1. Moving forward (forward) - from your fighting stance, first move your front foot forward (approximately 12 inches) and then move your rear foot an equal distance.

2. Moving backward (backward) - from your fighting stance, first move your rear foot backward (approximately 12 inches) and then move your front foot an equal distance.

3. Moving right (sidestep right) - from your fighting stance, first move your right foot to the right (approximately 12 inches) and then move your left foot an equal distance.

4. Moving left (sidestep left) - from your fighting stance, first move your left foot to the left (approximately 12 inches) and then move your right foot an equal distance.

Practice shadowboxing with these four movements for 10 to 15 minutes a day in front of a full-length mirror. In a couple weeks, your footwork should be quick, balanced, and natural.

Circling Right and Left

Circling footwork is a slightly more advanced, where you will use your front leg as a pivot point. This type of movement can also be used defensively to evade an overwhelming combination assault or to counter strike the opponent from a strategic angle. Strategic circling can be performed from either an orthodox or southpaw stance.

Circling left (from a left stance) - this means you'll be moving your body around the ring in a clockwise direction. From a left stance, step approximately shoulder distance to the left with your

Boxing Styles and Techniques: Making Sense of It All

left foot. Then use your left leg as a pivot point and wheel your entire right leg to the left (in the direction of an arc) until the correct boxing stance and positioning is acquired.

Circling right (from a left stance) - this means you'll be moving your body around the ring in a counter clockwise direction. From a left stance, with your body traveling in the direction of an arc, step approximately shoulder distance to the right with your right foot, then pivot your left foot until the correct stance and positioning is acquired.

When performing circular footwork, remember the footwork rule of thumb still applies: *Always move the foot closest to the direction you want to go first, and let the other foot follow an equal distance.*

Boxing Techniques

Mastery of basic boxing punches is a necessity for boxing domination. This includes the following techniques:

- **Left Jab**
- **Straight Right**
- **Left Hook**
- **Right Hook**
- **Left Uppercut**
- **Right Uppercut**

Boxing Domination

The Jab

The jab is a foundation technique for boxers and mixed martial artists. This punch is thrown from your front hand and it has a quick snap when delivered.

1. Start off in a fighting stance with both of your hands held up in the guard position. Remember to keep both of your fists lightly clenched with both of your elbows pointing to the ground.
2. To perform the punch, simultaneously step forward and snap your front arm out.
3. Remember to turn your fist so it lands in a horizontal position.
4. When delivering the punch, remember not to lock out your arm, as this will have a "pushing effect".
5. Quickly retract your arm back to the starting position.

Boxing Styles and Techniques: Making Sense of It All

Straight Right

The straight right is considered the heavy artillery of punches and it's thrown from your rear arm. To execute the punch, perform the following steps:

1. Begin from the fighting stance.
2. Quickly twist your rear hips and shoulders forward as you snap your rear arm. Proper weight transfer is of paramount importance. You must shift your weight from your rear foot to your lead leg as you throw the punch.
3. Turn your fist so it lands in a horizontal position.
4. Avoid overextending the blow or exposing your chin during its execution.
5. Don't lock out your arm when throwing the punch. Let punch sink in before retracting it to the starting position.

Hook Punch

The hook is another devastating punch that's also one of the most difficult to master. This punch can be performed from either your front or rear hand and it can be thrown at both high and low targets.

To perform either the lead or rear hook punch, follow these steps:

1. Start in a fighting stance.

2. Quickly and smoothly, raise your elbow up so that your arm is parallel to the ground while simultaneously torquing your shoulder, hip, and foot into the target.

3. When delivering the punch, be certain your arm is bent at least ninety degrees and that your wrist and forearm are kept straight throughout the movement.

4. Your fist is positioned vertically and your elbow should be locked when contact is made with the opponent.

5. Return back to the starting position.

Boxing Styles and Techniques: Making Sense of It All

Uppercut Punch

The uppercut is a another powerful punch that can also be delivered from both the lead and rear arm. To perform the technique, follow these steps:

1. Begin from the fighting stance.
2. Next, drop your shoulder and bend your knees.
3. Quickly, lift up and drive your fist upward and into the target.
4. Your palm should be facing you when contact is made with the opponent. To avoid any possible injury, keep your wrists straight.
5. Make certain that the punch has a tight arc and that you avoid any and all "winding up" motions. A properly executed uppercut should be a tight punch and should feel like an explosive jolt.
6. Return back to the fighting stance.

Boxing Attributes

For a boxer to be effective in the ring, he or she must possess certain basic fighting attributes. Attributes are both physical and mental qualities that maximize your fighting skills.

For example, speed, power, timing, non telegraphic movement, rhythm, coordination, accuracy, balance, and mental toughness are just a few boxing attributes that must be present if any boxer is to be effective in the ring.

Let's explore a few attributes necessary for boxing domination: speed, power, timing, balance, and non telegraphic movement.

Speed

You need to be fast. While some athletes are blessed with great speed, the good news is that with proper training you can obtain it rather quickly. In my book Speed Boxing Secrets, I covered in great detail the importance of boxing speed training. Speed development for boxing is actually comprised of two training components:

- **Visual reflexes and recognition speed**
- **Movement speed**

Each link in the speed chain represents a particular component or micro-attribute of speed that should be trained and developed to maximize your speed performance in the ring..

Power

Power refers to the amount of impact force you can generate when hitting your opponent. Fortunately, the power of your punch is not necessarily predicated on your size and strength. A relatively small person can generate devastating knockout power if he or she has the proper training.

Boxing Styles and Techniques: Making Sense of It All

Timing

Timing refers to your ability to execute a boxing technique at the optimum moment. There are two types of timing: defensive and offensive. Defensive timing is the time between the opponent's punch and your defensive response to that attack. Offensive timing is the time between your recognition of a target opening and your offensive response to that opening.

Balance

Effectively knockout power requires substantial follow-through while maintaining your balance. Balance is your ability to maintain equilibrium while stationary or moving. You can maintain perfect balance only through controlling your center of gravity, mastering boxing mechanics, and maintaining proper skeletal alignment.

Non Telegraphic Movement

The element of surprise is an invaluable tool in boxing. Successfully landing a knockout blow requires that you don't forewarn your opponent of your intentions. Clenching your teeth, widening your eyes, cocking your fist, and tensing your neck or shoulders are just a few common telegraphic cues that will negate the element of surprise.

One of the best ways to prevent telegraphic movement is to maintain a poker face prior to executing your punch. Make it a habit to always avoid any and all facial expressions when working out in the gym and fighting in the ring.

Boxing Styles

Once a fighter acquires these fundamental boxing skills, he or she will naturally have developed their own style of fighting. In most cases, it's a gradual process resulting from hours of training and practicing. Depending on the fighters strengths and weaknesses, their fighting style will be one of four conventional forms of fighting. Let's take a look at each one.

Conventional Boxing Styles

Conventional Boxing generally refers to a "textbook style" of fighting. Essentially, it's a boxer who adheres to the fundamentals of his or her sport by using what other fighters have done before them. There are four conventional boxing styles that are used. They include the following:

- **Inside Fighter**
- **Outside Fighter**
- **Slugger**
- **Boxer-Puncher**

Despite the fact these styles of boxing differ from each other, they are still classified as conventional methods of ring fighting. Moreover, these four conventional boxing styles are not mutually exclusive. For example, some boxers might employ a subtle combination of conventional styles. For example, there are fighters who might be a combination of Outside Fighting with the Slugger style of boxing.

Let's take a closer look at each conventional style by starting with the Inside Fighter.

Boxing Styles and Techniques: Making Sense of It All

The Inside Fighter

The Inside Fighter tries to eliminate his opponent's reach, timing and distancing by overwhelms him with constant forward pressure. Inside Fighters are also highly skilled with evasion movements like bobbing, weaving, ducking, and slipping. This style of boxing allows the fighter to get inside their opponent's long-range attacks and counter with a variety of close-quarter punches such as hooks, uppercuts, and shovel hooks. Finally, a well-seasoned Inside Fighter is likened to a tank - designed and built to withstand a tremendous amount of physical punishment.

The Outside Fighter

The Outside Fighter is the antithesis of the Inside Fighter. He or she continually tries to maintain a strategic distance gap from their opponent by using long-range punches, such as jabs and straights. The success of an Outside Fighter is also predicated on lightning-quick log range punches accompanied with extremely quick footwork. As you can imagine, Outside Fighters often win boxing matches by points decisions rather than by knockout blow.

Muhammad Ali was the quintessential Outside Fighter.

Boxing Domination

The Slugger

In the sport of boxing, the Slugger is likened to a brawler who often lacks finesse and footwork. His combat philosophy is "the best defense is a powerful and overwhelming offense." Nevertheless, the Slugger is a very dangerous opponent in the ring, easily capable of knocking out his adversary with just a single punch. For this reason alone, Sluggers are sometimes confused with Inside Fighters.

Compared to the Outside Fighter, Sluggers have difficulty keeping up with mobile opponents and also tend to deliver fewer punching combinations. Many Sluggers are also known for delivering telegraphic punches, but lord have mercy if just one blow makes contact. Lights out folks!

How would you classify the legendary Rocky Marciano? Slugger? In-Fighter? Or perhaps a human wrecking machine!

Boxing Styles and Techniques: Making Sense of It All

The Boxer-Puncher

The Boxer-Puncher is a hybrid or combination of both the Outside Fighter and Slugger. Meaning, he or she possesses punching speed, including both combination and counter-punching skills. Generally the Boxer-Puncher will also possess better defense skills accompanied with bone-rattling Slugger punching power.

Boxer-Punchers also tend to be more aggressive than an Outside Fighter. However, the boxer-puncher often lacks the footwork, mobility, and defensive expertise of the pure style boxer.

Unconventional Boxing Styles

Now that you have a basic understanding of conventional boxing styles, it's time to take a look at **unconventional styles** and methods of fighting. Essentially, an unconventional boxing style is one that intentionally abandons the fundamental techniques of boxing in favor of a more unpredictable approach to fighting in the ring. The operative word is "unpredictable." Some famous unconventional boxers include:

- **Prince Naseem Hamed**
- **Floyd "Money" Mayweather Jr.**
- **Guillermo "El Chacal" Rigondeaux**
- **Sergio "Maravilla" Martinez**
- **Joshua Clottey**

Advantages of Unconventional Boxing

There are some darn good reasons why you might want to add an unconventional style of boxing into your repertoire. Here are just a few good reasons why you might want to consider it.

YOUR ODDS OF WINNING SKYROCKET

By integrating just a few elements of unconventional boxing into your repertoire, you'll dramatically increase your odds of winning the boxing match.

PREPARATION ROADBLOCK

It's difficult for any boxer to prepare to fight against an unconventional boxing style. For example, when your opponent trains to fight you, he will have a very difficult time finding a sparring partner who can replicate your unusual and unorthodox style of boxing. The bottom line is, others can't copy your style of boxing.

GETTING NOTICED IN THE SPORT

Boxing and mixed martial arts is a big business and fans expect to be entertained. Textbook boxing styles accompanied with a dull or robotic personality is the beginning of the end for any aspiring boxer. If you want to succeed, you'll need to stand out from all of the others in the sport. Remember, an unconventional boxer is someone who performs differently from his competition; he or she is an exciting fighter who can generate big crowds.

MAKING BOXING HISTORY

By showcasing a refreshingly distinctive and effective fighting style, you'll make a name for yourself that will outlive your boxing career. In fact, your boxing performance and career highlights will be forever immortalized in the annals of boxing history.

Boxing Styles and Techniques: Making Sense of It All

You can't get anymore unconventional than Prince Naseem Hamed (right).

What This Book Can Do For You

The goal of this book is to teach you a variety of unconventional boxing styles that you can seamlessly integrate with your current conventional style of fighting.

You'll discover that some unorthodox styles will work well for you, while others don't. The key is to pick the techniques that do work for you and discard the ones that don't serve your needs. To paraphrase the late Bruce Lee, "Absorb what is useful, reject what is useless and adopt what is clearly your own."

However, keep in mind, these unique fighting styles must first be practiced and developed under real-time sparring conditions before you attempting to use them during an actual match.

Finally, integrating some or all of my unconventional fighting styles into your boxing program or fight strategy can be done in some

Boxing Domination

of the following ways:

- **Alternate During the Round:** You can alternate conventional and unconventional styles (sparingly and or intermittently) during the course of a 3-minute round of boxing.

- **Alternate Every Other Round:** Or you might want to switch up conventional and unconventional styles of fighting every round. For example: Round 1: Conventional boxing, Round 2: Unconventional boxing, Round 3: Conventional boxing, etc.

Chapter 1
Bait and Smash

Boxing Domination

Chapter 1: Bait and Smash

You Bait and then Smash!

The **Bait and Smash** is deceptive counter punching technique that will confuse the most seasoned boxer. In this method of attack, the boxer offers the opponent an enticing bait (i. e. creating an intentional opening designed to lure a punch).

The Boxer-Puncher and Outside Fighter will find the Bait and Smash fairly easy to add to their repertoire of fighting tricks. While Inside Fighters and Sluggers will find it challenging because they are generally uncomfortable fighting at long range. Nevertheless, it can be developed and ultimately mastered with sufficient sparring practice.

How to Apply the Bait and Smash

A common technique for the Bait and Smash is wide hand guard positioning, as if to say, "Come on, take your best shot!" Once the opponent takes the bait, the boxer swiftly executes a preplanned and perfectly timed counter attack. Proponents of this unconventional boxing strategy argue that it forces the opponent to commit himself to a decided action and offers you the opportunity to observe his speed, strategy and style of fighting.

The Bait and Smash method should always first be practiced and developed under sparring conditions before applying it in an actual boxing or MMA match. Moreover, you must make certain that you have the necessary recognition speed to be able to identify, intercept, and counter the opponent's initial attack (i.e., if your opponent has exceptional jabbing speed). The best way to ensure your success with the Bait and Smash is to practice with a sparring partner that has exceptional punching speed. Practice, practice, practice!

Depending if you are a boxer or mixed martial artists, there are two primary counter punches for the Bait and Smash technique. Let's take a look at them.

Bait and Smash (for Boxing)

Boxing has specific rules related to punching techniques. For example, it's illegal to strike the opponent with an open glove, the inside of the glove, your wrist, inner forearm, and the back or side of your hand.

In fact, every punch must be landed with the front of your fist (this is why the back fist and palm strike are illegal in boxing). Therefore, your counterpunch for the Bait and Smash is either be a jab or straight right.

Chapter 1: Bait and Smash

Bait and Smash Boxing Demonstration

Step 1: The boxer (right) opens his guard, offering a wide hand positioning to draw his opponent's attack.

Step 2: The opponent takes the bait and executes a jab. The defender (right) parries the blow with his opposite hand.

Boxing Domination

Step 3: The Boxer immediately counters with a quick jab to the head.

Step 4: He follows up with a straight right.

Chapter 1: Bait and Smash

Bait and Smash (for Mixed Martial Arts)

Mixed martial arts permit you to strike with the back of the hand. Accordingly, the Bait and Smash counterpunch can either be a back fist, jab or straight right.

Step 1: The fighter (left) opens his guard, offering a wide hand positioning to draw his opponent's attack.

Step 2: The opponent takes the bait and attacks.

Boxing Domination

Step 3: The defender quickly parries his opponent's attack.

Step 4: The fighter counters with either a jab or back fist punch.

Chapter 1: Bait and Smash

Step 5: Fortunately, mixed martial artists are permitted to strike with the back of their hand. Pictured here, the back fist strike is used in the bait and smash technique.

Boxing Domination

Chapter 2
The Roundabout

Boxing Domination

Chapter 2: The Roundabout

The Art of Confidence Killing

The **Roundabout** is progressive form of attacking your opponent in the ring and it always involves more than one offense technique. Do not, however, confuse the Roundabout with its superior cousin, the combination attack.

The goal of the Roundabout is simple - to irritate, annoy, and force your opponent to second guess both his identification and perception of a real attack. For all intents and purposes, the Roundabout is the *quintessential confidence killer* for your opponent.

Again, the Boxer-Puncher and Outside Fighter will find the Roundabout easy to learn. While Inside Fighters and Sluggers will find it a bit more challenging (it's outside their fighting range). Nevertheless, it can be developed and ultimately mastered with sufficient sparring practice.

How to Apply the Roundabout Technique

The Roundabout builds through stages. The initial punch is not the coup de grace, i.e., the knockout punch. In fact, in many Roundabouts the initiating technique is not even a punch, but one of any number of feints or other deceptions designed to open the opponent up for the follow-up blow.

Even when the initial technique is an actual punch, it serves merely as a set-up for the finishing blow or a combination of finishing blows. In boxing matches, the initiating technique sets up or accumulates valuable points, wears down the opponent, and opens them up to more devastating blows. The Roundabout can also be especially effective under sparring conditions.

Be forewarned, the initiating technique in a Roundabout must be delivered with maximum speed and determination or it will be ignored or countered with viciousness. Consider the sheer lunacy of attempting a half-baked feint or fake against a well-seasoned opponent. Your technique must appear legitimate or it won't sell itself to the opponent. Remember, you have to "sell it."

Those boxers who have trained excessively in the use of feints, should limit their use to just outside the opponent's reach. A feint from this distance does not create a risk as it would in-fighting range. If the opponent fails to take the bait of a Roundabout or reacts offensively, you're still at a relatively safe distance.

Chapter 2: The Roundabout

Roundabout Demonstration

Step 1: *The two boxers square off with each other.*

Step 2: *The boxer on the right begins his roundabout attack with a low line fake to his opponent's body.*

Boxing Domination

Step 3: The opponent goes for the fake by parrying low with his right hand. The boxer (right) builds on this opening with a lead hook to the head.

CAUTION: Remember that your initiating punch should NOT be a fully committed blow. Instead, it should be any number of feints or other deceptions designed to open the opponent up. In this photo, the fighter (right) demonstrates a fully committed blow that can easily be countered by the opponent.

Chapter 3
Cover and Crush

Boxing Domination

Chapter 3: Cover and Crush

Closing In on Him!

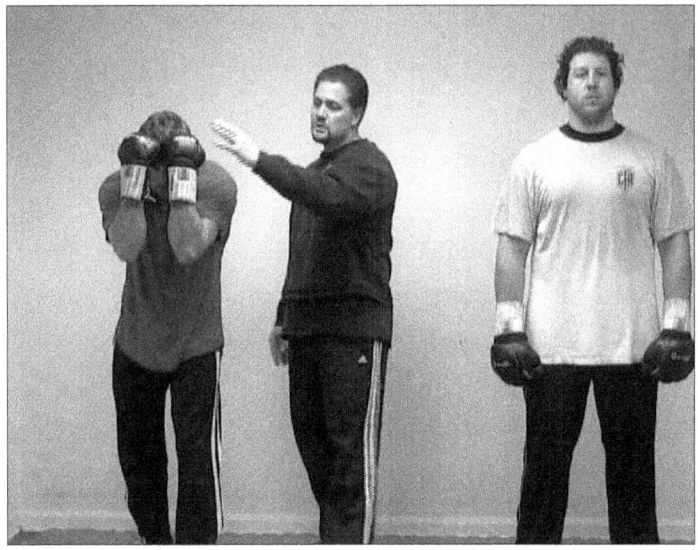

The **Cover and Crush** technique is used to close the distance gap between long fighting and inside fighting boxing ranges. It can be used for both offensive and defensive situations. For example, if your opponent is attacking you, you can still move in on him and close the distance gap with the Cover and Crush technique.

The concept of the Cover and Crush is similar to Greek military battle formation of the phalanx. As a military formation, the phalanx was practically unstoppable. It functioned as both a slow moving battering ram and a massive meat grinder, designed for direct, head-on, bloody combat.

Inside Fighters and Sluggers can easily adapt to Cover and Crush style of boxing, and readily add it to their repertoire of boxing skills. However, the Boxer-Puncher and Outside Fighters will find the Cover and Crush a bit more challenging. Again, it can still be developed and ultimately mastered with sufficient sparring practice.

Boxing Domination

How to Apply the Cover and Crush

To perform the Cover and Crush, follow these steps:

1. Maintain a solid boxing stance, with your bodyweight evenly distributed.
2. Keep both gloves up and in front of your face, above your eyebrow line.
3. Keep both of your elbows and forearms close and tight. Don't worry about your opponent's linear punches (i.e., jab, straight right) won't penetrate through forearms, there simply isn't enough space for his blows to get through.
4. Look directly forward, through both of your gloves. Never close your eyes or look down at your feet. Remember, you must always be able to see your opponent.
5. Next, use your footwork skills to advance at your adversary, while maintaining a solid fighting stance. Keep in mind that strong, powerful leg muscles will be a big advantage with this technique.
6. Once you have closed the distance gap on your opponent and have acquired the in-fighting range, attack your opponent with tight uppercuts to his chin. Keep your uppercuts quick, explosive and non telegraphic. Under no circumstances should you wind up your punch.

Chapter 3: Cover and Crush

Cover and Crush Demonstration

Step 1: The boxers square off with each other.

Step 2: The boxer (left) assumes the cover and crush posture and begins to charge his opponent. The opponent attempts to keep him back with a flurry of blows.

41

Boxing Domination

Step 3: The boxer keeps his elbows and forearms close and tight while maintaining eye contact with his opponent.

Step 4: With advancing forward pressure, the boxer closes the distance gap and works his way inside his opponent's arms.

Chapter 3: Cover and Crush

Step 5: Once he's acquired the inside fighting range, he attacks his opponent with a tight uppercut to his chin.

Step 6: When performed correctly, the result can be a devastating one punch knockout.

Boxing Domination

Chapter 4
The Steamroller

Boxing Domination

Chapter 4: The Steamroller

Controlling the Fight

Of all the unorthodox boxing techniques featured in this book, the **Steamroller** requires the greatest amount of skill and practice to master.

The objective of the Steamroller is to temporarily control your opponent's arm preceding your attack. Simply put, your goal is to slap down (thereby controlling) the opponent's hand guard as you advance forward. This can be tricky for the boxer because the rules of boxing prohibit holding down your opponent hand guard while hitting him at the same time. So, to pull this off, it must look like a slap and not a hold or immobilization technique. The good news is, with lots of sparring practice, you can easily pull this off in a boxing match.

The success of the Steamroller technique is predicated on synchronizing your footwork with your hand movement. It requires you to be explosive and dynamic with both your hands and feet so you can quickly close the distance gap quickly and efficiently.

47

Boxing Domination

How to Apply the Steamroller for Boxing

To perform the Steamroller for boxing, follow these steps:

1. Maintain a solid boxing stance, with your bodyweight evenly distributed.
2. When your opponent is within arms reach of your gloves, explode forward and slap his lead hand down with your front hand.
3. This instant his glove drops down, hit him with either a jab or straight right.
4. It's critical that your footwork is non-telegraphic and timed perfectly with your slapping hand.
5. Remember to use the Steamroller judiciously as well as sparingly. Too much of any single domination technique must always be avoided.

Advice For Boxers (Pro or Amateur)

As I mentioned earlier, boxing has specific rules related to holding your opponent's body and limbs. You must remember to release the slap before you make contact with either your jab or straight right. If you practice with your sparring partner, you'll get the technique down to an exact science. I promise.

Chapter 4: The Steamroller

How to Apply the Steamroller for Mixed Martial Arts

To perform the Steamroller for Mixed Martial Arts, follow these steps:

1. Maintain a solid fighting stance, with your bodyweight evenly distributed.
2. When your opponent is within arms reach of your gloves, explode forward and slap his lead hand down with your front hand.
3. This instant his glove drops down, roll your other hand over his boxing glove.
4. Continue this type of rolling hand motion over the opponent's hand guard as you advance forward.
5. It's critical that your footwork is non-telegraphic and timed perfectly with your slapping hands.
6. Remember, in order for the Steamroller to be unpredictable, it must be used sparingly during the fight.

Advice For Mixed Martial Arts (MMA)

While the Steamroller is a great agitation technique in Boxing, it's a virtual wrecking machine in Mixed Martial Arts. Since holding and trapping your opponent is permitted in mixed martial arts, you can unleash the Steamroller with full effect - a barrage and flurry of slaps, traps and hits.

Boxing Domination

Steamroller Demonstration for MMA

The following pictures demonstrate the Steamroller tactic applied in Mixed Martial Arts.

Step 1: The MMA fighter (left) defends against his opponent's jab.

Step 2: Next, he parries and covers his opponent's jab with his lead hand.

Chapter 4: The Steamroller

Step 3: The fighter explodes forward and slaps the jab down with his front hand, while closing the distance gap.

Step 4: In the event the opponent backs away, he keeps the pressure on with advancing footwork and more hand trapping action.

Boxing Domination

Step 5: When done correctly, the Steamroller creates a flurry of hand movement that overwhelms and confuses the opponent.

Step 6: The fighter has temporarily trapped his opponent's hands and acquired the inside fighting range.

Chapter 5
Catch Me Now

Boxing Domination

Chapter 5: Catch Me Now

A Game of Cat and Mouse

Catch Me Now is the ultimate boxing methodology for distracting, frustrating and demoralizing your opponent. It's also a great way to get the crowd of spectators out of their seats and on their feet. However, it's also the riskiest tactic to use in the ring.

Some people might call Catch Me Now showboating, but it's a damn good method for driving your opponent mad. This unconventional fighting method is not a single technique, but a combination of taunting movements designed to irritate your foe. The key is maintaining a constant and unpredictable state of confusion for the opponent.

Like all boxing domination tactics, you must be judicious when applying the Catch Me Now. If you abuse it by using it too frequently or applying it at the wrong time, you can get yourself knocked out. Therefore, it must be used with caution. The Catch Me Now techniques include some of the following:

Boxing Domination

Dropping Your Hands Down

This is the most insulting of all gestures in boxing. Essentially, dropping you hands down implies that your opponent isn't a threat worth protecting yourself. In nine out of ten cases, your opponent will become infuriated at the gesture and come right after you like a bull in a china shop. Therefore, dropping your hands must only be done under one of the following circumstances:

1. The opponent is outside striking range and unable to reach you with a punch.
2. The opponent is physically exhausted and doesn't have the energy to attack you.
3. If you're a mixed martial artist, be certain you are outside the opponent's kicking range.

Bolo Punching

The Bolo Punch is a deceptive and audacious boxing move designed to distract your opponent from a real attack. Essentially, the punch looks like a long swinging uppercut (resembling an underhand softball throw) that would make any boxing coach or fighting purist cringe.

Several well-know boxers have recognized the utility of the Bolo Punch and have used it with much success. They include, Sugar Ray Leonard, Roy Jones Jr., and Joe Calzaghe.

Generally, the Bolo Punch is delivered with the rear hand in a long wind-up motion or chambering action. The goal is to be telegraphic and draw the opponent's attention to the blow. Once he takes bait and anticipates the Bolo Punch, attack him instead with your lead hand (i.e., jab or hook).

Chapter 5: Catch Me Now

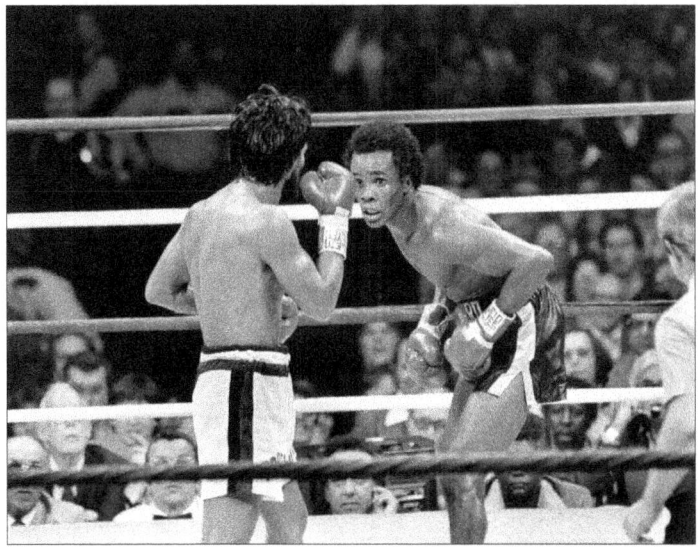

Taunting Body Language

Taunting Body Language includes a variety of facial expressions and body language that provoke and challenge your opponent to lose his cool in the ring. They include some of the following:

- Sticking your head forward, as if daring your opponent to hit you.
- Smiling or smirking after getting hit by the opponent.
- Showing disgust by pulling down your eyebrows accompanied with a wrinkled nose.
- Enlarging your eyes, as if daring him to hit you.
- Raising your eyebrows are if you are shocked by your opponent's poor performance.
- Gaping mouth (be certain you are outside of striking range).
- Shaking your head back and forth after he misses with a blow.

Boxing Domination

- Excessively frowning at him.
- Shrugging your shoulders (best used when dropping your hands down).
- Placing both of your hands on your hips as if you're waiting for him to do something interesting.
- Beckon the opponent with your front hand and encourage him to come closer or follow you around the ring.

Slipping Movements (both inside and outside fighting ranges)

Slipping is a quick defensive maneuver that permits you to avoid the opponent's linear blow (jab, straight right) without stepping out of range. Safe and effective slipping requires precise timing and is accomplished by quickly snapping the head and upper torso sideways (right or left) or backwards to avoid the oncoming punch. One of the greatest advantages to slipping is that it frees your hands so that you can simultaneously counter your opponent.

There are three ways to slip. They include the following:

- **Slipping right** - start from a stance and quickly sway your head and upper torso to the right to avoid the assailant's blow. Quickly counter or return to the starting position.
- **Slipping left** - start from a stance and quickly sway your head and upper torso to the left to avoid the assailant's linear blow. Quickly counter or return to the starting position.
- **Slipping back (also called the snap back)** - start from a stance and quickly snap your head back far enough to avoid being hit. Quickly counter or return to the starting position.

Chapter 5: Catch Me Now

Proactive Ducking

Ducking is the process of dropping your body down and forward to avoid the opponent's blows or to attack his body. Generally, ducking is used as a reactive defensive move against the opponent's attack.

However, you can also use Ducking as an annoying proactive move (i.e., you have no intention of attacking the opponent) to irritant to the opponent. Imagine the opponent's visual irritation when you are unnecessarily ducking throughout the duration of a round. Best of all, the opponent has no idea when you ducking will actually be executed with a tactical purpose.

The body mechanics for both ducking punches or executing body shots are the same. To perform the technique properly, apply the following steps:

- From your stance, keep both hands up, back straight, and both knees bent.

- Keep your eyes focused on your opponent and allow your torso to drop down.

- If you are reacting to a blow, be certain to drop down so the oncoming punch misses the top of your head.

- To return to the starting position, using your knees, quickly lift your body up back to a fighting stance.

- When performing ducking, avoid bending at the waist or looking down at the ground.

Bobbing and Weaving

The Bob and Weave are popular defensive techniques that can be integrated with the Catch Me Now tactic. Essentially, you are circling and leaning with the head while also changing the position of your upper body.

The bob drops your body down from the waist, and the weave pulls you to the other side. Bobbing and weaving works great for boxers in the ring, but it should be used with extreme caution in mixed martial arts matches, where both knee strikes and kicks are permitted.

Exaggerated Feinting and Fakes

Feints and fakes are setup techniques that can draw either offensive or defensive reactions from the opponent, thereby opening him up for a real blow. These and other deceptions are commonly used in boxing and sparring matches to "test" the opponent, wear him down both physically and psychologically, and ultimately score valuable points. Examples of Exaggerated Feinting include some of the following:

- Pretending to punch the opponent to draw his defensive reaction.
- Pretending to advance forward through quick forward body leaning.
- Pretending to attack a body target but then hitting his head instead.
- Leaning excessively to one side (not to be confused with slipping).
- Pretending to move to the right, but then moving to the left.
- Pretending to move to the left, but then moving to the right.

Chapter 5: Catch Me Now

Floor Stomping

Stomping on the canvass can also be a real irritant to your opponent. Not only can this serve as an auditory distraction, but it can also enhance your jab's punching power. Floor stomping is best used in combination with Taunting Facial Expressions and Hand Gestures.

Dancing Around the Opponent

When used carefully, Dancing Around the Opponent can help the boxer during a match by winning over the crowd and irritating the opponent. The important question isn't if you should use it, but "when" you can safely apply it during a match.

Much of this will depend on two important factors:

1. The opponent's current state of mind.
2. The opponent's current physical status (i.e., is he fatigued, noticeably exhausted, injured, etc).

Combining Catch Me Now Techniques

Catch Me Now techniques can be performed individually or combined in unique ways. Here are just a few ways you can combine them into a fluid series of moves. Again, these are just some suggestions that you might want to take a look at. In the end, will ultimately determine what works best for you and your fighting style.

1. Dropping Your Hands Down with Slipping Movements.
2. Dancing Around the Opponent with Taunting Body Language.
3. Proactive Ducking with Bolo Punching.
4. Floor stomping with Bolo Punching.

Boxing Domination

5. Dropping Your Hands Down with Taunting Body Language.
6. Proactive Ducking with Exaggerated Feinting and Fakes.
7. Exaggerated Feinting and Fakes with Bolo Punching.
8. Dropping your Hand Down Bolo Punching.
9. Slipping Movements with Exaggerated Feinting and Fakes.
10. Proactive Ducking with Taunting Body Language.

Catch Me Now Shadowboxing

Shadowboxing is the creative deployment of offensive and defensive boxing techniques against an imaginary opponent. It requires intense mental concentration, honest self-analysis, and a deep commitment to improving your fighting skills.

For someone on a tight budget, the good news is that shadowboxing is cheap. All you need is a full-length mirror and a place to work out. The mirror is vital. It functions as a critic, your

Chapter 5: Catch Me Now

personal boxing coach. If you're honest, the mirror will be too. It will point out every mistake - telegraphing, sloppy footwork, poor punching mechanics, and even lack of physical conditioning.

Traditional shadowboxing develops many fighting attributes like speed, balance, footwork, combination skills, sound form, and finesse. However, Catch Me Now Shadowboxing differs from conventional shadowboxing because it places full emphasis on unconventional tactics throughout the duration of the drill.

In a nutshell, the goal of Catch Me Now Shadowboxing is to incorporate the unconventional tactics (i.e., dropping your hands down, bolo punching, taunting body language, floor stomping, dancing around the opponent, etc.) with convention methods (i.e., solid boxing stance, flawless punching mechanics, balanced footwork, etc.) for three minute rounds.

Also, get into the habit of videotaping your shadowboxing sessions. Critique your performance and identify the Catch Me Now tactics that work best for you and those that create unwanted vulnerabilities.

Finally, a good Catch Me Now Shadowboxing workout consists of at least three rounds lasting three minutes in duration.

Boxing Domination

Chapter 6
Boxing Domination Exercises

Boxing Domination

Chapter 6: Boxing Domination Exercises

Training to Dominate in the Ring

Now that we have covered the five major domination boxing styles, it's time to look at the different exercises that will allow you to practice and refine them. Let's begin with Domination Sparring.

Domination Sparring

Domination Sparring is, by far, the most important component of unconventional boxing training. Besides developing the many attributes necessary for boxing (courage, timing, distancing, accuracy, compound attack skills, etc.) it will also condition your body for the rigors of fighting.

In addition, domination sparring will also allow you to test which unorthodox styles work for you and others that don't. Moreover, unconventional sparring, on a regular basis, will also help minimize some of the fear associated with its inherent risks.

Boxing Domination

Remember to "test out" each one of the different unorthodox fighting styles, including:

- **Bait and Smash**
- **The Roundabout**
- **Cover and Crush**
- **The Steamroller**
- **Catch Me Now**

Sparring for boxing domination requires you to focus on being subtle and unpredictable with your opponent. Avoid being structured and formulaic. This can be tricky and especially frustrating when you are sparring with someone who is capable of quickly figuring you out.

They key is to alternate between conventional and unorthodox boxing methodologies. And don't forget to always move around with quick and economical footwork, regardless of your style of fighting.

NOTE: If you discover that your domination tactics provide very little threat to your opponent, and actually provokes him to attack with greater intensity, you can always fall back to your tried and true foundational boxing skills. This will ultimately keep your opponent guessing and allow you to eventually go back to utilizing unorthodox attacks.

However, if you still find domination sparring too frustrating or unproductive, you should consider training with someone who is less skilled than you. In fact, domination sparring with someone of lesser ability will provide you with the opportunity to work on your skills, without the risk and fear of getting injured. Finally, strive for at least six rounds of domination sparring, lasting three minutes in duration.

Chapter 6: Boxing Domination Exercises

Domination Shadowboxing

As I mentioned in the previous chapter, Shadowboxing is the creative deployment of offensive and defensive boxing techniques against an imaginary opponent. It requires intense mental concentration, honest self-analysis, and a deep commitment to improving your fighting skills.

For someone on a tight budget, the good news is that shadowboxing is cheap. All you need is a full-length mirror and a place to work out. The mirror is vital. It functions as a critic, your personal boxing coach. If you're honest, the mirror will be too. It will point out every mistake - telegraphing, sloppy footwork, poor punching mechanics, and even lack of physical conditioning.

Traditional shadowboxing develops many fighting attributes like speed, balance, footwork, combination skills, sound form, and finesse. However, domination shadowboxing differs from conventional shadowboxing because it places full emphasis on unorthodox tactics throughout the duration of the drill.

The goal is to incorporate the following tactics into your training session. Again, they include:

- **Bait and Smash**
- **The Roundabout**
- **Cover and Crush**
- **The Steamroller**
- **Catch Me Now**

Also, get into the habit of videotaping your shadowboxing sessions. Critique your performance and identify the tactics that work for you and those that create unwanted and dangerous vulnerabilities. Finally, a good domination shadowboxing workout consists of at least five rounds lasting three minutes in duration.

Domination Double-End Bag Training

The double-end bag (also called a top and bottom bag, floor to ceiling ball, crazy bag, headache bag, and reflex bag) is tried and true for developing both reflexes and movement speed. When used correctly, it can also enhance your Catch Me Now fighting skills.

Double-end bags are small, inflatable lightweight round bags that are most often constructed of vinyl or leather. This unique training bag is suspended in the air using two durable elastic cables that anchor it to the ceiling and the floor.

They also come in a variety of different sizes including large (9 inches), medium (7 inches) and small (6 inches). The size of the double end bag matters. The smaller the bag, the more difficult it is to hit it when training. As a rule of thumb, beginners should always start off with a large size bag.

Be forewarned! The double-end bag requires a considerable amount of practice and a hell of a lot of patience. In fact, it's probably

Chapter 6: Boxing Domination Exercises

one of the most difficult pieces of boxing equipment to master.

For example, when you strike on the bag, it immediately reacts by swinging right back at you. In fact, the harder you hit the bag, the faster is rebounds. Therefore, to properly control the movement of the bag, you must strike it directly in the center. If you don't hit it dead center, it will bounce uncontrollably to the right or left.

Since double-end bag training is a popular form of working out, you can find just about every type of bag variation by surfing the Internet. However, be prepared, it can be a bit overwhelming as there are so many on the market.

Once you hang the double-end bag, the next important issue is making certain it is set at the proper height. One of the most common mistakes is setting the height of the bag too low. Be sure that your bag is set up so that you can effectively land head level shots. Essentially, the top of the double end bag should be level with your head.

To ensure the proper height you might have to adjust the length of the elastic rubber cables or bungee straps. This will most likely take a bit of experimentation and some trial and error, but the result will be worth the effort.

Since double-end bag training is structured around time and rounds, you should invest in a good workout timer. Boxers, mixed martial artists, and kick boxers will use workout timers to keep track of their time during their rounds.

Most workout timers will allow you to adjust your round lengths anywhere from 30 seconds to 9 minutes. Rest time can be set from 30 seconds to 5 minutes depending on your level of conditioning and training goals.

There are several professional timers sold on the market, and they vary in price. Some of them can be very pricey. However, there are numerous smartphone apps that replicate the same function and characteristics of an actual interval timer. These workout timer apps are convenient and very inexpensive. Your best bet is to search the Internet or your favorite app store for one that meets your specific needs.

Finally, a good double-end bag workout would consist of 5 three-minute rounds with a one minute rest period in between each round.

Domination Heavy Bag Training

As I discussed in my three part Heavy Bag book series, the heavy bag is a fantastic piece of training equipment that provides a full range of benefits for the boxer. Some include:
- Developing and sharpening your fighting skills.
- Conditioning your entire body for the rigors of intense fighting.
- Improving muscular endurance.
- Strengthening your bones, tendons, and ligaments for the

Chapter 6: Boxing Domination Exercises

demands of power punching.

- Conditioning your cardiovascular system.
- Relieving pent up stress.
- Channeling aggressive energy into a productive outlet.
- Developing several mental toughness attributes, such as instrumental aggression, immediate resilience, self-confidence, and attention control.

Surprisingly, the heavy bag can also be used for developing domination fighting tactics by applying Domination Interval Drills.

Domination Interval Drills

Any boxer worth his salt will tell you that heavy bag training is a delicate mixture of power, speed, timing, and pacing. However, the real secret to making the most of your heavy bag workout is to apply some of the different boxing domination tactics during your three-minute round on the bag.

This brings us to **Domination Interval Heavy Bag Training** which requires the boxer to alternate between periods of conventional techniques with unorthodox tactics.

For example, you begin by working on the bag with fundamentally solid punching and footwork skills, then incorporating a Bolo Punch, taunting body language, proactive ducking, bait and smash, etc. The domination style combinations you can create are endless. If your imaginative in your training, you'll understanding what I'm talking about.

Boxing Domination

Domination Interval Workout Examples

For a typical three minute round of boxing, you can structure your Domination Interval workout many different ways. Here are just two examples:

The 30/15 Domination Interval Workout

This is a 3 minute round that includes the following: 30 seconds conventional fighting - 15 seconds domination tactics - 30 seconds conventional fighting - 15 seconds domination tactics - 30 seconds conventional fighting - 15 domination tactics - 30 seconds conventional fighting - 15 domination tactics.

The 30/30 Domination Interval Workout

This is a 3 minute round that includes the following: 30 seconds conventional fighting - 30 seconds domination fighting - 30 seconds conventional fighting - 30 seconds domination fighting - 30 seconds conventional fighting - 30 seconds domination fighting.

Chapter 6: Boxing Domination Exercises

Domination Punching Mitt Training

The punching mitt or focus pad is an exceptional piece of training equipment that can be used by anyone. By placing the mitts at various angles and levels, you can perform every conceivable punch. Punching mitts also develops both offensive and defensive skills, accuracy, speed, target recognition, target selection, timing, and condition your entire body for boxing.

Punching mitts are constructed of durable leather designed to withstand tremendous punishment. Compared to other pieces of equipment, the mitts are relatively inexpensive. However, an effective workout requires two mitts (one for each hand).

Your training partner (called the feeder) plays a vital role in your punching mitt workout by controlling the techniques you execute and the cadence of delivery. The intensity of your workouts will depend largely upon his or her ability to manipulate the mitts and push you to your limit. I often tell my students that a good mitt feeder is one step ahead of his training partner, whereas a great mitt feeder is two steps ahead of his partner.

Boxing Domination

When training with your partner, give them constructive feedback and let them know how he or she is doing. Remember, communication is vital during your workout sessions. Also, try to avoid remaining stationary. Get into the habit of constantly moving around with quick, economical steps.

To truly benefit from any punching mitt workout, you must learn to concentrate intensely throughout the entire session. You must block out both internal and external distractions. Try to visualize the mitt as a living, breathing opponent, not an inanimate target. This type of visualization will make the difference between a poor workout and a great training session. You also might want to draw small Xs on the mitts. This practice will improve your focus and concentration and help you develop accurate striking techniques.

Using the punching mitts for domination boxing requires a highly skilled feeder who knows how to integrate both conventional and unorthodox methods into your workout session.

For example, during the course of a three minute round your partner might require you to deliver clean punches followed by a Bolo punch and some exaggerated fakes and feints. If he knows what he or she is doing, the options are limitless.

Finally, domination punching mitt workouts are usually conducted for three minute rounds with a one minute rest. You can have feed your partner set combination patterns or he can give you arbitrary targets. Much of it will really depend on his skill level. If you are going for time, strive for at least 5 rounds lasting three minutes in duration.

Chapter 6: Boxing Domination Exercises

Boxing Domination

Chapter 7
Boxing Domination Workout Programs

Boxing Domination

Chapter 7: Boxing Domination Workout Programs

How To Create a Boxing Domination Workout Program

Now, we are going to take all of the knowledge from the previous chapters and put them into a solid program. In this chapter, I'm going to teach you how to create a 21-day boxing domination program. However, before we begin, you must be certain that your program meets the following criteria.

- **Realistic** - your training should be as real as possible. It should include drills and exercises that replicate the exact conditions of boxing or mixed martial arts.

- **Simple** - your training should be easy to put into action. It should not require time-consuming preparation or expensive or complex equipment.

- **Specific** - your training should meet specific training goals. This might be a micro goal, such as developing a specific unconventional boxing technique.

- **Quantifiable** - you must be able to accurately measure your progress in training. Performance measurement is motivational and helps you stay committed to your goals. It also useful for identifying exercises that are not helping you reach your personal objectives.

Let's Get Started...

Let me start by saying, there's no single boxing domination program that works for everyone. Since each of us has different goals, skill levels and time line, it's up to you to identify your needs and personalize your training accordingly. The bottom line is, only you can determine what works best for you.

Boxing Domination

As you might imagine, there are many different ways to set up a boxing domination program. In fact, some of you might want to first consult with your coach, trainer, or instructor prior to setting up a routine.

How to do it...

STEP 1: IDENTIFY YOUR "CONVENTIONAL" BOXING STYLE:

Are you an Inside Fighter, Outside Fight, Slugger, or Boxer-Puncher? Now is the time to take a personal inventory or your style of fighting. Once you have determined what type of "conventional" fighter you are, move on to Step 2.

STEP 2: IDENTIFY YOUR DOMINATION MICRO GOAL:

For this example, let's say your goal is to specifically develop the Bait and Smash technique and ultimately add it to your boxing repertoire.

STEP 3: SELECT THE TWO BOXING STYLES YOU WANT TO INTEGRATE:

Now, choose one style from each of the two boxing styles categories (one from domination and one from conventional) listed below. In this example, let's say you are a Slugger who wants to add the Bait and Smash technique to your repertoire.

Conventional Boxing Styles:

- **Inside Fighter**
- **Outside Fighter**
- **Slugger**
- **Boxer-Puncher**

Chapter 7: Boxing Domination Workout Programs

Domination Boxing Styles:

- **Bait and Smash**
- **Roundabout**
- **Cover and Crush**
- **The Steamroller**
- **Catch Me Now**

STEP 4: DETERMINE YOUR TRAINING FREQUENCY:

Next, decide how many days per week you want to train. To avoid injury and prevent overtraining, refrain from domination boxing everyday. Between two to four times per week yields the best results.

STEP 5: CREATE YOUR PROGRAM:

Now that you have identified your convention style of fighting (Slugger), the domination style micro goal (Bait and Smash), and determined your training frequency (three times per week), it's time to structure it around a period of one week. In this example, you will train three times per week with a micro goal of developing the Bait and Smash technique. See example below:

- **Monday** - Slugger Training (standard training)
- **Tuesday** - rest
- **Wednesday** - Bait and Smash Training
- **Thursday** - rest
- **Friday** - Slugger & Bait and Smash Training
- **Saturday** - rest
- **Sunday** - rest

Boxing Domination

Sample 21-Day Domination Boxing Programs

What follows are sample 21-day boxing domination programs. You will also find that some programs require you to train twice per week and others require three times. Again, these are just examples of what you can do. In the final analysis, it's up to you to decide what works best for you.

PROGRAM #1: Here's a 21-day boxing domination program for an **Inside Fighter** focusing on the **Bait and Smash** style.

Week 1:

- Monday - Bait and Smash Training
- Tuesday - rest
- Wednesday - Inside Fighting Training
- Thursday - rest
- Friday - Bait and Smash Training
- Saturday - rest
- Sunday - rest

Week 2:

- Monday - Inside Fighting Training
- Tuesday- rest
- Wednesday- Inside Fighting Training
- Thursday - rest
- Friday - Bait and Smash Training
- Saturday- rest
- Sunday - rest

Chapter 7: Boxing Domination Workout Programs

Week 3:

- Monday - Inside Fighting Training
- Tuesday - Bait and Smash Training
- Wednesday - rest
- Thursday - rest
- Friday - Inside Fighting Training
- Saturday - rest
- Sunday - rest

PROGRAM #2: Here's a 21-day boxing domination program for a **Boxer-Puncher** focusing on the **Steamroller** style.

Week 1:

- Monday - Boxer-Puncher Training
- Tuesday - rest
- Wednesday - Steamroller Training
- Thursday - rest
- Friday - Boxer-Puncher Training
- Saturday - rest
- Sunday - rest

Week 2:

- Monday - Steamroller Training
- Tuesday - rest
- Wednesday - Boxer-Puncher Training
- Thursday - Steamroller Training
- Friday - Boxer-Puncher Training
- Saturday and Sunday - rest

Boxing Domination

Week 3:

- Monday - Boxer-Puncher Training
- Tuesday - rest
- Wednesday - Boxer-Puncher Training
- Thursday - Steamroller Training
- Friday - Boxer-Puncher Training
- Saturday- rest
- Sunday - rest

PROGRAM #3: Here's a 21-day boxing domination program for a **Slugger** focusing on the **Roundabout** style.

Week 1:

- Monday - Slugger Training
- Tuesday - rest
- Wednesday - Slugger Training
- Thursday - rest
- Friday - Roundabout Training
- Saturday and Sunday - rest

Week 2:

- Monday - Roundabout Training
- Tuesday - Slugger Training
- Wednesday - rest
- Thursday - rest
- Friday - Slugger Training
- Saturday and Sunday - rest

Chapter 7: Boxing Domination Workout Programs

Week 3:

- Monday - Slugger Training
- Tuesday - Roundabout Training
- Wednesday - rest
- Thursday - Roundabout Training
- Friday - Slugger Training
- Saturday - rest
- Sunday - rest

PROGRAM #4: Here's a 21-day boxing domination program for an **Outside Fighter** focusing on the **Cover and Crush** style.

Week 1:

- Monday - Cover and Crush Training
- Tuesday - rest
- Wednesday - Outside Fighter Training
- Thursday - rest
- Friday - Outside Fighter Training
- Saturday and Sunday - rest

Week 2:

- Monday - Out-Fighter Training
- Tuesday - Cover and Crush Training
- Wednesday - rest
- Thursday - Out-Fighter Training
- Friday - Cover and Crush Training
- Saturday and Sunday - rest

Boxing Domination

Week 3:

- Monday - Cover and Crush Training
- Tuesday - rest
- Wednesday - Outside Fighter Training
- Thursday - Cover and Crush Training
- Friday - Outside Fighter Training
- Saturday - rest
- Sunday - rest

PROGRAM #5: Here's a 21-day boxing domination program for an **Inside Fighter** focusing on the **Catch Me Now** style.

Week 1:

- Monday - Inside Fighter Training
- Tuesday - rest
- Wednesday - Catch Me Now Training
- Thursday - rest
- Friday - Inside Fighter Training
- Saturday and Sunday - rest

Week 2:

- Monday - Catch Me Now Training
- Tuesday - rest
- Wednesday - Inside Fighter Training
- Thursday - Inside Fighter Training
- Friday - Catch Me Now Training
- Saturday and Sunday - rest

Chapter 7: Boxing Domination Workout Programs

Week 3:

- Monday - Inside Fighter Training
- Tuesday - Catch Me Now Training
- Wednesday - Inside Fighter Training
- Thursday - rest
- Friday - Inside Fighter Training
- Saturday - rest
- Sunday - rest

PROGRAM #6: Here's a 21-day boxing domination for a **Slugger** focusing on both **Bait and Smash** and **Catch Me Now** styles.

Week 1:

- Monday - Slugger Training
- Tuesday - rest
- Wednesday - Bait and Smash Training
- Thursday - rest
- Friday - Slugger Training
- Saturday and Sunday - rest

Week 2:

- Monday - Slugger Training
- Tuesday - rest
- Wednesday - Bait and Smash Training
- Thursday - Slugger Training
- Friday - Catch Me Now Training
- Saturday and Sunday - rest

Boxing Domination

Week 3:
- Monday - Slugger Training
- Tuesday - rest
- Wednesday - Bait and Smash and Catch Me Now Training
- Thursday - Slugger Training
- Friday - Slugger Training
- Saturday - rest
- Sunday - rest

Finding the Right Training Partner

As I discussed earlier, many of these exercises can be performed individually, while others will require the assistance of a training partner, instructor or coach.

A good training partner should motivate, challenge and push you to your limits. He or she doesn't have to share the same goals as you do, but they must be willing to help you reach your full potential. Your training partner or coach should also be somewhat familiar with the various drills.

While a good training partner can be a major asset, having a bad one can be a major liability. Be exceptionally careful who you choose to train with you. When looking for a training parter, try to avoid the following personality types:

- **The conversationalist** - someone who talks too much and often disrupts the training intensity.
- **The challenger** - someone who is naturally argumentative and tries to test your knowledge and patience.
- **The ego tripper** - someone who will do anything to prove

just how tough he is. He usually enjoys full-contact drills and likes to injure others during training.

- **The insecure one** - someone who is hesitant to participate in training full-contact drills and exercises.
- **The know-it-all** - someone who thinks he knows anything and everything about boxing or mixed martial arts.
- **The dilettante** - someone who doesn't understand the importance of domination training, and therefore doesn't fully commit himself to the program.

Finally, remember that a good training partner or coach is there to evaluate your performance during your workouts. Listen carefully to what he has to say. A good coach, for example, will be brutally honest and tell you what you are doing correctly and what you are doing wrong. Learn to put your ego aside and heed his advice.

Safety When Training

Safety precautions must always be taken when engaged in boxing domination training. Remember, a serious injury can set you back for weeks and even months. Don't make the mistake of letting your ego or laziness get the best of you. Learn to be safety-conscious. Here are a few suggestions to help minimize the possibilities of injury when training:

- Buy the best boxing equipment that you can afford.
- Know the proper way to use training equipment.
- Regularly inspect your equipment for wear and defects.
- Avoid ego-driven training partners or coaches.
- Be especially aware when training with someone of superior skill or experience.
- Always warm up before training.

Boxing Domination

- Drink plenty of water during training sessions to avoid dehydration.
- Be cautious when performing training drills for the first time.

It's also a good idea to have a first-aid kit nearby. A first-aid kit is intended for both minor and major injuries. The kit should be kept in a well-sealed box away from children. Don't forget to write down the emergency number for your local hospital or medical clinic on the box. Most first-aid kits can be purchased at your local drugstore. Each kit should contain cotton wool and hydrogen peroxide for cleaning cuts, tweezers, scissors, triangular bandages, alcohol swabs, adhesive tape, adhesive bandages, antibiotic ointment, sterile pads, gauze bandages, and elastic bandages for sprains and for elbow and knee injuries.

Avoiding Overtraining & Burnout

Burnout is defined as a negative emotional state acquired by physical overtraining. Some symptoms of burnout include physical illness, boredom, anxiety, disinterest in training, and general sluggish behavior. Whether you are a beginner or expert, you're susceptible to burnout. Here are a few suggestions to help avoid burnout in your training:

1. Make your workouts intense but enjoyable.
2. Vary your training routine (i.e., hard day/easy day routine).
3. Train to different types of music.
4. Pace yourself during your workouts - don't try to do it all in one day.
5. Listen to your body- if you don't feel up to training, skip a day.
6. Work out in different types of environments.

Chapter 7: Boxing Domination Workout Programs

7. Use different types of training equipment.
8. Workout with different training partners.
9. Keep accurate records of your training routine.
10. Vary the intensity of your training throughout your workout.

Keeping Track of Your Training

In order to reap the full benefits of training, you need to keep track of your workouts and monitor your progress. Monitoring your training will give you a wide range of benefits, including:

- Help determine if you making progress in your training.
- The ability to effectively alter your training program.
- Track your rate of progress.
- Stay interested and motivated.
- Break through performance plateaus.

Two of the best tools for keeping track of your training progress are: the training journal and video footage. Let's take a look at each one.

The Training Journal

Record keeping is one of the most important and often neglected aspects of boxing domination training. Try to make it a habit to keep accurate records of your workouts in a personal journal. This type of record keeping is important for some of the following reasons:

- It will help you monitor your progress.
- It will keep you organized.
- It will inspire, motivate and remind you to stick to your goals.
- It helps prevent potential injuries.
- It will help you guard against overtraining.

Boxing Domination

- If you are learning new skills, it accelerates the learning process.
- It gives you valuable training information that can be analyzed.
- It helps you determine which boxing styles are unproductive.
- It helps you determine which activities are helpful and productive.

When making entries into your journal, don't forget to include some of the following important details:

- The date and time you trained.
- The boxing style you are training.
- The types of drills or exercises you performed.
- The number or sets, reps you performed for each exercise or drill.
- The number or rounds and minutes per round you performed for each drill or exercise.
- The feelings you experienced before, during, and after your workout.
- Your overall mood.
- Concerns you have about your current training.
- Comments, ideas and observations made by your coach, training partner or instructor.

Videotaping Your Workouts

If you really want to actually see your progress, videotape your workouts. The video will provide you with a more accurate picture of what you are doing in your training. You will be able to observe

Chapter 7: Boxing Domination Workout Programs

mistakes and recognize your strengths and weaknesses. The video footage will also motivate you to train harder. Remember to date each videotape or video clip; later on you will be able to compare and see marked improvements in your boxing domination skills.

Boxing Domination

Glossary

A

accuracy—The precise or exact projection of force. Accuracy is also defined as the ability to execute a combative movement with precision and exactness.

adaptability—The ability to physically and psychologically adjust to new or different conditions or circumstances of combat.

advanced first-strike tools—Offensive techniques that are specifically used when confronted with multiple opponents.

aerobic exercise—Literally, "with air." Exercise that elevates the heart rate to a training level for a prolonged period of time, usually 30 minutes.

affective preparedness – One of the three components of preparedness. Affective preparedness means being emotionally, philosophically, and spiritually prepared for the strains of combat. See cognitive preparedness and psychomotor preparedness.

aggression—Hostile and injurious behavior directed toward a person.

aggressive response—One of the three possible counters when assaulted by a grab, choke, or hold from a standing position. Aggressive response requires you to counter the enemy with destructive blows and strikes. See moderate response and passive response.

aggressive hand positioning—Placement of hands so as to imply aggressive or hostile intentions.

agility—An attribute of combat. One's ability to move his or her body quickly and gracefully.

Boxing Domination

amalgamation—A scientific process of uniting or merging.

ambidextrous—The ability to perform with equal facility on both the right and left sides of the body.

anabolic steroids – synthetic chemical compounds that resemble the male sex hormone testosterone. This performance-enhancing drug is known to increase lean muscle mass, strength, and endurance.

analysis and integration—One of the five elements of CFA's mental component. This is the painstaking process of breaking down various elements, concepts, sciences, and disciplines into their atomic parts, and then methodically and strategically analyzing, experimenting, and drastically modifying the information so that it fulfills three combative requirements: efficiency, effectiveness, and safety. Only then is it finally integrated into the CFA system.

anatomical striking targets—The various anatomical body targets that can be struck and which are especially vulnerable to potential harm. They include: the eyes, temple, nose, chin, back of neck, front of neck, solar plexus, ribs, groin, thighs, knees, shins, and instep.

anchoring – The strategic process of trapping the assailant's neck or limb in order to control the range of engagement during razing.

assailant—A person who threatens or attacks another person.

assault—The threat or willful attempt to inflict injury upon the person of another.

assault and battery—The unlawful touching of another person without justification.

assessment—The process of rapidly gathering, analyzing, and accurately evaluating information in terms of threat and danger. You can assess people, places, actions, and objects.

attack—Offensive action designed to physically control, injure, or kill another person.

Glossary

attack by combination (ABC) - One of the five methods of attack. See compound attack.

attack by drawing (ABD) - One of the five methods of attack. A method of attack predicated on counterattack.

attitude—One of the three factors that determine who wins a street fight. Attitude means being emotionally, philosophically, and spiritually liberated from societal and religious mores. See skills and knowledge.

attributes of combat—The physical, mental, and spiritual qualities that enhance combat skills and tactics.

awareness—Perception or knowledge of people, places, actions, and objects. (In CFA, there are three categories of tactical awareness: criminal awareness, situational awareness, and self-awareness.)

B

balance—One's ability to maintain equilibrium while stationary or moving.

blading the body—Strategically positioning your body at a 45-degree angle.

blitz and disengage—A style of sparring whereby a fighter moves into a range of combat, unleashes a strategic compound attack, and then quickly disengages to a safe distance. Of all sparring methodologies, the blitz and disengage most closely resembles a real street fight.

block—A defensive tool designed to intercept the assailant's attack by placing a non-vital target between the assailant's strike and your vital body target.

body composition—The ratio of fat to lean body tissue.

body language—Nonverbal communication through posture,

gestures, and facial expressions.

body mechanics—Technically precise body movement during the execution of a body weapon, defensive technique, or other fighting maneuver.

body tackle – A tackle that occurs when your opponent haphazardly rushes forward and plows his body into yours.

body weapon—Also known as a tool, one of the various body parts that can be used to strike or otherwise injure or kill a criminal assailant.

burn out—A negative emotional state acquired by physically over- training. Some symptoms include: illness, boredom, anxiety, disinterest in training, and general sluggishness.

C

cadence—Coordinating tempo and rhythm to establish a timing pattern of movement.

cardiorespiratory conditioning—The component of physical fitness that deals with the heart, lungs, and circulatory system.

centerline—An imaginary vertical line that divides your body in half and which contains many of your vital anatomical targets.

choke holds—Holds that impair the flow of blood or oxygen to the brain.

circular movements—Movements that follow the direction of a curve.

close-quarter combat—One of the three ranges of knife and bludgeon combat. At this distance, you can strike, slash, or stab your assailant with a variety of close-quarter techniques.

cognitive development—One of the five elements of CFA's mental

Glossary

component. The process of developing and enhancing your fighting skills through specific mental exercises and techniques. See analysis and integration, killer instinct, philosophy, and strategic/tactical development.

cognitive exercises—Various mental exercises used to enhance fighting skills and tactics.

cognitive preparedness – One of the three components of preparedness. Cognitive preparedness means being equipped with the strategic concepts, principles, and general knowledge of combat. See affective preparedness and psychomotor preparedness.

combat-oriented training—Training that is specifically related to the harsh realities of both armed and unarmed combat. See ritual-oriented training and sport-oriented training.

combative arts—The various arts of war. See martial arts.

combative attributes—See attributes of combat.

combative fitness—A state characterized by cardiorespiratory and muscular/skeletal conditioning, as well as proper body composition.

combative mentality—Also known as the killer instinct, this is a combative state of mind necessary for fighting. See killer instinct.

combat ranges—The various ranges of unarmed combat.

combative utility—The quality of condition of being combatively useful.

combination(s)—See compound attack.

common peroneal nerve—A pressure point area located approximately four to six inches above the knee on the midline of the outside of the thigh.

composure—A combative attribute. Composure is a quiet and focused mind-set that enables you to acquire your combative agenda.

Boxing Domination

compound attack—One of the five conventional methods of attack. Two or more body weapons launched in strategic succession whereby the fighter overwhelms his assailant with a flurry of full speed, full-force blows.

conditioning training—A CFA training methodology requiring the practitioner to deliver a variety of offensive and defensive combinations for a 4-minute period. See proficiency training and street training.

contact evasion—Physically moving or manipulating your body to avoid being tackled by the adversary.

Contemporary Fighting Arts—A modern martial art and self-defense system made up of three parts: physical, mental, and spiritual.

conventional ground-fighting tools—Specific ground-fighting techniques designed to control, restrain, and temporarily incapacitate your adversary. Some conventional ground fighting tactics include: submission holds, locks, certain choking techniques, and specific striking techniques.

coordination—A physical attribute characterized by the ability to perform a technique or movement with efficiency, balance, and accuracy.

counterattack—Offensive action made to counter an assailant's initial attack.

courage—A combative attribute. The state of mind and spirit that enables a fighter to face danger and vicissitudes with confidence, resolution, and bravery.

creatine monohydrate—A tasteless and odorless white powder that mimics some of the effects of anabolic steroids. Creatine is a safe body-building product that can benefit anyone who wants to increase their strength, endurance, and lean muscle mass.

Glossary

criminal awareness—One of the three categories of CFA awareness. It involves a general understanding and knowledge of the nature and dynamics of a criminal's motivations, mentalities, methods, and capabilities to perpetrate violent crime. See situational awareness and self-awareness.

criminal justice—The study of criminal law and the procedures associated with its enforcement.

criminology—The scientific study of crime and criminals.

cross-stepping—The process of crossing one foot in front of or behind the other when moving.

crushing tactics—Nuclear grappling-range techniques designed to crush the assailant's anatomical targets.

D

deadly force—Weapons or techniques that may result in unconsciousness, permanent disfigurement, or death.

deception—A combative attribute. A stratagem whereby you delude your assailant.

decisiveness—A combative attribute. The ability to follow a tactical course of action that is unwavering and focused.

defense—The ability to strategically thwart an assailant's attack (armed or unarmed).

defensive flow—A progression of continuous defensive responses.

defensive mentality—A defensive mind-set.

defensive reaction time—The elapsed time between an assailant's physical attack and your defensive response to that attack. See offensive reaction time.

demeanor—A person's outward behavior. One of the essential

Boxing Domination

factors to consider when assessing a threatening individual.

diet—A lifestyle of healthy eating.

disingenuous vocalization—The strategic and deceptive utilization of words to successfully launch a preemptive strike at your adversary.

distancing—The ability to quickly understand spatial relationships and how they relate to combat.

distractionary tactics—Various verbal and physical tactics designed to distract your adversary.

double-end bag—A small leather ball hung from the ceiling and anchored to the floor with bungee cord. It helps develop striking accuracy, speed, timing, eye-hand coordination, footwork and overall defensive skills.

double-leg takedown—A takedown that occurs when your opponent shoots for both of your legs to force you to the ground.

E

ectomorph—One of the three somatotypes. A body type characterized by a high degree of slenderness, angularity, and fragility. See endomorph and mesomorph.

effectiveness—One of the three criteria for a CFA body weapon, technique, tactic, or maneuver. It means the ability to produce a desired effect. See efficiency and safety.

efficiency—One of the three criteria for a CFA body weapon, technique, tactic, or maneuver. It means the ability to reach an objective quickly and economically. See effectiveness and safety.

emotionless—A combative attribute. Being temporarily devoid of human feeling.

Glossary

endomorph—One of the three somatotypes. A body type characterized by a high degree of roundness, softness, and body fat. See ectomorph and mesomorph.

evasion—A defensive maneuver that allows you to strategically maneuver your body away from the assailant's strike.

evasive sidestepping—Evasive footwork where the practitioner moves to either the right or left side.

evasiveness—A combative attribute. The ability to avoid threat or danger.

excessive force—An amount of force that exceeds the need for a particular event and is unjustified in the eyes of the law.

experimentation—The painstaking process of testing a combative hypothesis or theory.

explosiveness—A combative attribute that is characterized by a sudden outburst of violent energy.

F

fear—A strong and unpleasant emotion caused by the anticipation or awareness of threat or danger. There are three stages of fear in order of intensity: fright, panic, and terror. See fright, panic, and terror.

feeder—A skilled technician who manipulates the focus mitts.

femoral nerve—A pressure point area located approximately 6 inches above the knee on the inside of the thigh.

fighting stance—Any one of the stances used in CFA's system. A strategic posture you can assume when face-to-face with an unarmed assailant(s). The fighting stance is generally used after you have launched your first-strike tool.

Boxing Domination

fight-or-flight syndrome—A response of the sympathetic nervous system to a fearful and threatening situation, during which it prepares your body to either fight or flee from the perceived danger.

finesse—A combative attribute. The ability to skillfully execute a movement or a series of movements with grace and refinement.

first strike—Proactive force used to interrupt the initial stages of an assault before it becomes a self-defense situation.

first-strike principle—A CFA principle that states that when physical danger is imminent and you have no other tactical option but to fight back, you should strike first, strike fast, and strike with authority and keep the pressure on.

first-strike stance—One of the stances used in CFA's system. A strategic posture used prior to initiating a first strike.

first-strike tools—Specific offensive tools designed to initiate a preemptive strike against your adversary.

fisted blows – Hand blows delivered with a clenched fist.

five tactical options – The five strategic responses you can make in a self-defense situation, listed in order of increasing level of resistance: comply, escape, de-escalate, assert, and fight back.

flexibility—The muscles' ability to move through maximum natural ranges. See muscular/skeletal conditioning.

focus mitts—Durable leather hand mitts used to develop and sharpen offensive and defensive skills.

footwork—Quick, economical steps performed on the balls of the feet while you are relaxed, alert, and balanced. Footwork is structured around four general movements: forward, backward, right, and left.

fractal tool—Offensive or defensive tools that can be used in more than one combat range.

fright—The first stage of fear; quick and sudden fear. See panic and terror.

full Beat – One of the four beat classifications in the Widow Maker Program. The full beat strike has a complete initiation and retraction phase.

G

going postal - a slang term referring to a person who suddenly and unexpectedly attacks you with an explosive and frenzied flurry of blows. Also known as postal attack.

grappling range—One of the three ranges of unarmed combat. Grappling range is the closest distance of unarmed combat from which you can employ a wide variety of close-quarter tools and techniques. The grappling range of unarmed combat is also divided into two planes: vertical (standing) and horizontal (ground fighting). See kicking range and punching range.

grappling-range tools—The various body tools and techniques that are employed in the grappling range of unarmed combat, including head butts; biting, tearing, clawing, crushing, and gouging tactics; foot stomps, horizontal, vertical, and diagonal elbow strikes, vertical and diagonal knee strikes, chokes, strangles, joint locks, and holds. See punching range tools and kicking range tools.

ground fighting—Also known as the horizontal grappling plane, this is fighting that takes place on the ground.

guard—Also known as the hand guard, this refers to a fighter's hand positioning.

guard position—Also known as leg guard or scissors hold, this is a ground-fighting position in which a fighter is on his back holding his opponent between his legs.

H

half beat – One of the four beat classifications in the Widow

Boxing Domination

Maker Program. The half beat strike is delivered through the retraction phase of the proceeding strike.

hand immobilization attack (HIA) - One of the five methods of attack. A method of attack whereby the practitioner traps his opponent's limb or limbs in order to execute an offense attack of his own.

hand positioning—See guard.

hand wraps—Long strips of cotton that are wrapped around the hands and wrists for greater protection.

haymaker—A wild and telegraphed swing of the arms executed by an unskilled fighter.

head-hunter—A fighter who primarily attacks the head.

heavy bag—A large cylindrical bag used to develop kicking, punching, or striking power.

high-line kick—One of the two different classifications of a kick. A kick that is directed to targets above an assailant's waist level. See low-line kick.

hip fusing—A full-contact drill that teaches a fighter to "stand his ground" and overcome the fear of exchanging blows with a stronger opponent. This exercise is performed by connecting two fighters with a 3-foot chain, forcing them to fight in the punching range of unarmed combat.

histrionics—The field of theatrics or acting.

hook kick—A circular kick that can be delivered in both kicking and punching ranges.

hook punch—A circular punch that can be delivered in both the punching and grappling ranges.

I

Glossary

impact power—Destructive force generated by mass and velocity.

impact training—A training exercise that develops pain tolerance.

incapacitate—To disable an assailant by rendering him unconscious or damaging his bones, joints, or organs.

initiative—Making the first offensive move in combat.

inside position—The area between the opponent's arms, where he has the greatest amount of control.

intent—One of the essential factors to consider when assessing a threatening individual. The assailant's purpose or motive. See demeanor, positioning, range, and weapon capability.

intuition—The innate ability to know or sense something without the use of rational thought.

J

jeet kune do (JKD) - "Way of the intercepting fist." Bruce Lee's approach to the martial arts, which includes his innovative concepts, theories, methodologies, and philosophies.

jersey Pull - Strategically pulling the assailant's shirt or jacket over his head as he disengages from the clinch position.

joint lock—A grappling-range technique that immobilizes the assailant's joint.

K

kick—A sudden, forceful strike with the foot.

kicking range—One of the three ranges of unarmed combat. Kicking range is the furthest distance of unarmed combat wherein you use your legs to strike an assailant. See grappling range and punching range.

kicking-range tools—The various body weapons employed in the kicking range of unarmed combat, including side kicks, push kicks, hook kicks, and vertical kicks.

killer instinct—A cold, primal mentality that surges to your consciousness and turns you into a vicious fighter.

kinesics—The study of nonlinguistic body movement communications. (For example, eye movement, shrugs, or facial gestures.)

kinesiology—The study of principles and mechanics of human movement.

kinesthetic perception—The ability to accurately feel your body during the execution of a particular movement.

knowledge—One of the three factors that determine who will win a street fight. Knowledge means knowing and understanding how to fight. See skills and attitude.

L

lead side -The side of the body that faces an assailant.

leg guard—See guard position.

linear movement—Movements that follow the path of a straight line.

low-maintenance tool—Offensive and defensive tools that require the least amount of training and practice to maintain proficiency. Low maintenance tools generally do not require preliminary stretching.

low-line kick—One of the two different classifications of a kick. A kick that is directed to targets below the assailant's waist level. (See

Glossary

high-line kick.)

lock—See joint lock.

M

maneuver—To manipulate into a strategically desired position.

MAP—An acronym that stands for moderate, aggressive, passive. MAP provides the practitioner with three possible responses to various grabs, chokes, and holds that occur from a standing position. See aggressive response, moderate response, and passive response.

martial arts—The "arts of war."

masking—The process of concealing your true feelings from your opponent by manipulating and managing your body language.

mechanics—(See body mechanics.)

mental attributes—The various cognitive qualities that enhance your fighting skills.

mental component—One of the three vital components of the CFA system. The mental component includes the cerebral aspects of fighting including the killer instinct, strategic and tactical development, analysis and integration, philosophy, and cognitive development. See physical component and spiritual component.

mesomorph—One of the three somatotypes. A body type classified by a high degree of muscularity and strength. The mesomorph possesses the ideal physique for unarmed combat. See ectomorph and endomorph.

mobility—A combative attribute. The ability to move your body quickly and freely while balanced. See footwork.

moderate response—One of the three possible counters when assaulted by a grab, choke, or hold from a standing position. Moderate response requires you to counter your opponent with a control and restraint (submission hold). See aggressive response and

Boxing Domination

passive response.

modern martial art—A pragmatic combat art that has evolved to meet the demands and characteristics of the present time.

mounted position—A dominant ground-fighting position where a fighter straddles his opponent.

muscular endurance—The muscles' ability to perform the same motion or task repeatedly for a prolonged period of time.

muscular flexibility—The muscles' ability to move through maximum natural ranges.

muscular strength—The maximum force that can be exerted by a particular muscle or muscle group against resistance.

muscular/skeletal conditioning—An element of physical fitness that entails muscular strength, endurance, and flexibility.

N

naked choke—A throat choke executed from the chest to back position. This secure choke is executed with two hands and it can be performed while standing, kneeling, and ground fighting with the opponent.

neck crush - A powerful pain compliance technique used when the adversary buries his head in your chest to avoid being razed.

neutralize—See incapacitate.

neutral zone—The distance outside the kicking range at which neither the practitioner nor the assailant can touch the other.

nonaggressive physiology—Strategic body language used prior to initiating a first strike.

nontelegraphic movement—Body mechanics or movements that do not inform an assailant of your intentions.

Glossary

nuclear ground-fighting tools—Specific grappling range tools designed to inflict immediate and irreversible damage. Nuclear tools and tactics include biting tactics, tearing tactics, crushing tactics, continuous choking tactics, gouging techniques, raking tactics, and all striking techniques.

O

offense—The armed and unarmed means and methods of attacking a criminal assailant.

offensive flow—Continuous offensive movements (kicks, blows, and strikes) with unbroken continuity that ultimately neutralize or terminate the opponent. See compound attack.

offensive reaction time—The elapsed time between target selection and target impaction.

one-mindedness—A state of deep concentration wherein you are free from all distractions (internal and external).

ostrich defense—One of the biggest mistakes one can make when defending against an opponent. This is when the practitioner looks away from that which he fears (punches, kicks, and strikes). His mentality is, "If I can't see it, it can't hurt me."

P

pain tolerance—Your ability to physically and psychologically withstand pain.

panic—The second stage of fear; overpowering fear. See fright and terror.

parry—A defensive technique: a quick, forceful slap that redirects an assailant's linear attack. There are two types of parries: horizontal and vertical.

passive response—One of the three possible counters when

assaulted by a grab, choke, or hold from a standing position. Passive response requires you to nullify the assault without injuring your adversary. See aggressive response and moderate response.

patience—A combative attribute. The ability to endure and tolerate difficulty.

perception—Interpretation of vital information acquired from your senses when faced with a potentially threatening situation.

philosophical resolution—The act of analyzing and answering various questions concerning the use of violence in defense of yourself and others.

philosophy—One of the five aspects of CFA's mental component. A deep state of introspection whereby you methodically resolve critical questions concerning the use of force in defense of yourself or others.

physical attributes—The numerous physical qualities that enhance your combative skills and abilities.

physical component—One of the three vital components of the CFA system. The physical component includes the physical aspects of fighting, such as physical fitness, weapon/technique mastery, and combative attributes. See mental component and spiritual component.

physical conditioning—See combative fitness.

physical fitness—See combative fitness.

positional asphyxia—The arrangement, placement, or positioning of your opponent's body in such a way as to interrupt your breathing and cause unconsciousness or possibly death.

positioning—The spatial relationship of the assailant to the assailed person in terms of target exposure, escape, angle of attack, and various other strategic considerations.

Glossary

postal attack - see going postal.

power—A physical attribute of armed and unarmed combat. The amount of force you can generate when striking an anatomical target.

power generators—Specific points on your body that generate impact power. There are three anatomical power generators: shoulders, hips, and feet.

precision—See accuracy.

preemptive strike—See first strike.

premise—An axiom, concept, rule, or any other valid reason to modify or go beyond that which has been established.

preparedness—A state of being ready for combat. There are three components of preparedness: affective preparedness, cognitive preparedness, and psychomotor preparedness.

probable reaction dynamics - The opponent's anticipated or predicted movements or actions during both armed and unarmed combat.

proficiency training—A CFA training methodology requiring the practitioner to execute a specific body weapon, technique, maneuver, or tactic over and over for a prescribed number of repetitions. See conditioning training and street training.

progressive indirect attack (PIA) – One of the five methods of attack. A progressive method of attack whereby the initial tool or technique is designed to set the opponent up for follow-up blows.

proxemics—The study of the nature and effect of man's personal space.

proximity—The ability to maintain a strategically safe distance from a threatening individual.

pseudospeciation—A combative attribute. The tendency to assign subhuman and inferior qualities to a threatening assailant.

Boxing Domination

psychological conditioning—The process of conditioning the mind for the horrors and rigors of real combat.

psychomotor preparedness—One of the three components of preparedness. Psychomotor preparedness means possessing all of the physical skills and attributes necessary to defeat a formidable adversary. See affective preparedness and cognitive preparedness.

punch—A quick, forceful strike of the fists.

punching range—One of the three ranges of unarmed combat. Punching range is the mid range of unarmed combat from which the fighter uses his hands to strike his assailant. See kicking range and grappling range.

punching-range tools—The various body weapons that are employed in the punching range of unarmed combat, including finger jabs, palm-heel strikes, rear cross, knife-hand strikes, horizontal and shovel hooks, uppercuts, and hammer-fist strikes. See grappling-range tools and kicking-range tools.

Q

qualities of combat—See attributes of combat.

quarter beat - One of the four beat classifications of the Widow Maker Program. Quarter beat strikes never break contact with the assailant's face. Quarter beat strikes are primarily responsible for creating the psychological panic and trauma when Razing.

R

range—The spatial relationship between a fighter and a threatening assailant.

range deficiency—The inability to effectively fight and defend in all ranges of combat (armed and unarmed).

Glossary

range manipulation—A combative attribute. The strategic manipulation of combat ranges.

range proficiency—A combative attribute. The ability to effectively fight and defend in all ranges of combat (armed and unarmed).

ranges of engagement—See combat ranges.

ranges of unarmed combat—The three distances (kicking range, punching range, and grappling range) a fighter might physically engage with an assailant while involved in unarmed combat.

raze – To level, demolish or obliterate.

razer – One who performs the Razing methodology.

razing – The second phase of the Widow Maker Program. A series of vicious close quarter techniques designed to physically and psychologically extirpate a criminal attacker.

razing amplifier - a technique, tactic or procedure that magnifies the destructiveness of your razing technique.

reaction dynamics—see probable reaction dynamics.

reaction time—The elapsed time between a stimulus and the response to that particular stimulus. See offensive reaction time and defensive reaction time.

rear cross—A straight punch delivered from the rear hand that crosses from right to left (if in a left stance) or left to right (if in a right stance).

rear side—The side of the body furthest from the assailant. See lead side.

reasonable force—That degree of force which is not excessive for a particular event and which is appropriate in protecting yourself or others.

Boxing Domination

refinement—The strategic and methodical process of improving or perfecting.

relocation principle—Also known as relocating, this is a street-fighting tactic that requires you to immediately move to a new location (usually by flanking your adversary) after delivering a compound attack.

repetition—Performing a single movement, exercise, strike, or action continuously for a specific period.

research—A scientific investigation or inquiry.

rhythm—Movements characterized by the natural ebb and flow of related elements.

ritual-oriented training—Formalized training that is conducted without intrinsic purpose. See combat-oriented training and sport-oriented training.

S

safety—One of the three criteria for a CFA body weapon, technique, maneuver, or tactic. It means that the tool, technique, maneuver or tactic provides the least amount of danger and risk for the practitioner. See efficiency and effectiveness.

scissors hold—See guard position.

scorching – Quickly and inconspicuously applying oleoresin capsicum (hot pepper extract) on your fingertips and then razing your adversary.

self-awareness—One of the three categories of CFA awareness. Knowing and understanding yourself. This includes aspects of yourself which may provoke criminal violence and which will promote a proper and strong reaction to an attack. See criminal awareness and situational awareness.

Glossary

self-confidence—Having trust and faith in yourself.

self-enlightenment—The state of knowing your capabilities, limitations, character traits, feelings, general attributes, and motivations. See self-awareness.

set—A term used to describe a grouping of repetitions.

shadow fighting—A CFA training exercise used to develop and refine your tools, techniques, and attributes of armed and unarmed combat.

sharking – A counter attack technique that is used when your adversary grabs your razing hand.

shielding wedge - a defensive maneuver used to counter an unarmed postal attack.

simple direct attack (SDA) – One of the five methods of attack. A method of attack whereby the practitioner delivers a solitary offenses tool or technique. It may involve a series of discrete probes or one swift, powerful strike aimed at terminating the encounter.

situational awareness—One of the three categories of CFA awareness. A state of being totally alert to your immediate surroundings, including people, places, objects, and actions. (See criminal awareness and self-awareness.)

skeletal alignment—The proper alignment or arrangement of your body. Skeletal alignment maximizes the structural integrity of striking tools.

skills—One of the three factors that determine who will win a street fight. Skills refers to psychomotor proficiency with the tools and techniques of combat. See Attitude and Knowledge.

slipping—A defensive maneuver that permits you to avoid an assailant's linear blow without stepping out of range. Slipping can be accomplished by quickly snapping the head and upper torso sideways (right or left) to avoid the blow.

snap back—A defensive maneuver that permits you to avoid an assailant's linear and circular blows without stepping out of range. The snap back can be accomplished by quickly snapping the head backward to avoid the assailant's blow.

somatotypes—A method of classifying human body types or builds into three different categories: endomorph, mesomorph, and ectomorph. See endomorph, mesomorph, and ectomorph.

sparring—A training exercise where two or more fighters fight each other while wearing protective equipment.

speed—A physical attribute of armed and unarmed combat. The rate or a measure of the rapid rate of motion.

spiritual component—One of the three vital components of the CFA system. The spiritual component includes the metaphysical issues and aspects of existence. See physical component and mental component.

sport-oriented training—Training that is geared for competition and governed by a set of rules. See combat-oriented training and ritual-oriented training.

sprawling—A grappling technique used to counter a double- or single-leg takedown.

square off—To be face-to-face with a hostile or threatening assailant who is about to attack you.

stance—One of the many strategic postures you assume prior to or during armed or unarmed combat.

stick fighting—Fighting that takes place with either one or two sticks.

strategic positioning—Tactically positioning yourself to either escape, move behind a barrier, or use a makeshift weapon.

Glossary

strategic/tactical development—One of the five elements of CFA's mental component.

strategy—A carefully planned method of achieving your goal of engaging an assailant under advantageous conditions.

street fight—A spontaneous and violent confrontation between two or more individuals wherein no rules apply.

street fighter—An unorthodox combatant who has no formal training. His combative skills and tactics are usually developed in the street by the process of trial and error.

street training—A CFA training methodology requiring the practitioner to deliver explosive compound attacks for 10 to 20 seconds. See condition ng training and proficiency training.

strength training—The process of developing muscular strength through systematic application of progressive resistance.

striking art—A combat art that relies predominantly on striking techniques to neutralize or terminate a criminal attacker.

striking shield—A rectangular shield constructed of foam and vinyl used to develop power in your kicks, punches, and strikes.

striking tool—A natural body weapon that impacts with the assailant's anatomical target.

strong side—The strongest and most coordinated side of your body.

structure—A definite and organized pattern.

style—The distinct manner in which a fighter executes or performs his combat skills.

stylistic integration—The purposeful and scientific collection of tools and techniques from various disciplines, which are strategically integrated and dramatically altered to meet three essential criteria: efficiency, effectiveness, and combative safety.

submission holds—Also known as control and restraint techniques, many of these locks and holds create sufficient pain to cause the adversary to submit.

system—The unification of principles, philosophies, rules, strategies, methodologies, tools, and techniques of a particular method of combat.

T

tactic—The skill of using the available means to achieve an end.

target awareness—A combative attribute that encompasses five strategic principles: target orientation, target recognition, target selection, target impaction, and target exploitation.

target exploitation—A combative attribute. The strategic maximization of your assailant's reaction dynamics during a fight. Target exploitation can be applied in both armed and unarmed encounters.

target impaction—The successful striking of the appropriate anatomical target.

target orientation—A combative attribute. Having a workable knowledge of the assailant's anatomical targets.

target recognition—The ability to immediately recognize appropriate anatomical targets during an emergency self-defense situation.

target selection—The process of mentally selecting the appropriate anatomical target for your self-defense situation. This is predicated on certain factors, including proper force response, assailant's positioning, and range.

target stare—A form of telegraphing in which you stare at the anatomical target you intend to strike.

Glossary

target zones—The three areas in which an assailant's anatomical targets are located. (See zone one, zone two and zone three.)

technique—A systematic procedure by which a task is accomplished.

telegraphic cognizance—A combative attribute. The ability to recognize both verbal and non-verbal signs of aggression or assault.

telegraphing—Unintentionally making your intentions known to your adversary.

tempo—The speed or rate at which you speak.

terminate—To kill.

terror—The third stage of fear; defined as overpowering fear. See fright and panic.

timing—A physical and mental attribute of armed and unarmed combat. Your ability to execute a movement at the optimum moment.

tone—The overall quality or character of your voice.

tool—See body weapon.

traditional martial arts—Any martial art that fails to evolve and change to meet the demands and characteristics of its present environment.

traditional style/system—See traditional martial arts.

training drills—The various exercises and drills aimed at perfecting combat skills, attributes, and tactics.

trap and tuck - A counter move technique used when the adversary attempts to raze you during your quarter beat assault.

U

unified mind—A mind free and clear of distractions and focused on the combative situation.

Boxing Domination

use of force response—A combative attribute. Selecting the appropriate level of force for a particular emergency self-defense situation.

V

viciousness—A combative attribute. The propensity to be extremely violent and destructive often characterized by intense savagery.

violence—The intentional utilization of physical force to coerce, injure, cripple, or kill.

visualization—Also known as mental visualization or mental imagery. The purposeful formation of mental images and scenarios in the mind's eye.

W

warm-up—A series of mild exercises, stretches, and movements designed to prepare you for more intense exercise.

weak side—The weaker and more uncoordinated side of your body.

weapon and technique mastery—A component of CFA's physical component. The kinesthetic and psychomotor development of a weapon or combative technique.

weapon capability—An assailant's ability to use and attack with a particular weapon.

webbing - The first phase of the Widow Maker Program. Webbing is a two hand strike delivered to the assailant's chin. It is called Webbing because your hands resemble a large web that wraps around the enemy's face.

widow maker – One who makes widows by destroying husbands.

widow maker program – A CFA combat program specifically designed to teach the law abiding citizen how to use extreme force

Glossary

when faced with immediate threat of unlawful deadly criminal attack. The Widow Maker program is divided into two phases or methodologies: Webbing and Razing.

Y

yell—A loud and aggressive scream or shout used for various strategic reasons.

Z

zero beat – One of the four beat classifications of the Widow Maker, Feral Fighting and Savage Street Fighting Programs. Zero beat strikes are full pressure techniques applied to a specific target until it completely ruptures. They include gouging, crushing, biting, and choking techniques.

zone one—Anatomical targets related to your senses, including the eyes, temple, nose, chin, and back of neck.

zone three—Anatomical targets related to your mobility, including thighs, knees, shins, and instep.

zone two—Anatomical targets related to your breathing, including front of neck, solar plexus, ribs, and groin.

Boxing Domination

About Sammy Franco

With over 30 years of experience, Sammy Franco is one of the world's foremost authorities on fighting. Highly regarded as a leading innovator in combat sciences, Mr. Franco was one of the premier pioneers in the field of combat instruction.

Sammy Franco is perhaps best known as the founder and creator of Contemporary Fighting Arts (CFA), a state-of-the-art offensive-based combat system that is specifically designed for real-world self-defense. CFA is a sophisticated and practical system of self-defense, designed specifically to provide efficient and effective methods to avoid, defuse, confront, and neutralize both armed and unarmed attackers.

Sammy Franco has frequently been featured in martial art magazines, newspapers, and appeared on numerous radio and television programs. Mr. Franco has also authored numerous books, magazine articles, and editorials, and has developed a popular library of instructional videos.

Sammy Franco's experience and credibility in the combat sciences is unequaled. One of his many accomplishments in this field includes the fact that he has earned the ranking of a Law Enforcement Master Instructor, and has designed, implemented, and taught officer survival training to the United States Border Patrol (USBP). He has instructed members of the US Secret Service, Military Special Forces, Washington DC Police Department, Montgomery County, Maryland Deputy Sheriffs, and the US Library of Congress Police. Sammy

Boxing Domination

Franco is also a member of the prestigious International Law Enforcement Educators and Trainers Association (ILEETA) as well as the American Society of Law Enforcement Trainers (ASLET) and he is listed in the "Who's Who Director of Law Enforcement Instructors."

Sammy Franco is a nationally certified Law Enforcement Instructor in the following curricula: PR-24 Side-Handle Baton, Police Arrest and Control Procedures, Police Personal Weapons Tactics, Police Power Handcuffing Methods, Police Oleoresin Capsicum Aerosol Training (OCAT), Police Weapon Retention and Disarming Methods, Police Edged Weapon Countermeasures and "Use of Force" Assessment and Response Methods.

Mr. Franco holds a Bachelor of Arts degree in Criminal Justice from the University of Maryland. He is a regularly featured speaker at a number of professional conferences and conducts dynamic and enlightening seminars on numerous aspects of self-defense and combat training.

On a personal level, Sammy Franco is an animal lover, who will go to great lengths to assist and rescue animals. Throughout the years, he's rescued everything from turkey vultures to goats. However, his most treasured moments are always spent with his beloved German Shepherd dogs.

For more information about Mr. Franco and his unique Contemporary Fighting Arts system, you can visit his website at: **SammyFranco.com** or follow him on twitter **@RealSammyFranco**

Other Books by Sammy Franco

SPEED BOXING SECRETS
A 21-Day Program to Hitting Faster and Reacting Quicker in Boxing and Mixed Martial Arts
by Sammy Franco

Speed Boxing Secrets: A 21-Day Program to Hitting Faster and Reacting Quicker in Boxing and Mixed Martial Arts is a comprehensive speed acceleration program made for anyone who wants to dramatically improve their fighting speed in a short period of time. When used correctly, this simple speed development program will double your boxing speed in as little as 21 days. 8.5 x 5.5, paperback, photos, illus, 150 pages.

POWER BOXING WORKOUT SECRETS
A 21-Day Program to Becoming a Devastating Knockout Puncher in Boxing and Mixed Martial Arts
by Sammy Franco

Power Boxing Workout Secrets: A 21-Day Program to Becoming a Devastating Knockout Puncher in Boxing and Mixed Martial Arts is a unique power development program made for fighters who want to be champions by dramatically increasing their power and explosiveness in the ring. When used correctly, this comprehensive power program will double your knockout power and fighting explosiveness in as little as 21 days. 8.5 x 5.5, paperback, photos, illus, 160 pages.

HEAVY BAG TRAINING
For Boxing, Mixed Martial Arts and Self-Defense
(Heavy Bag Training Series Book 1)
by Sammy Franco

The heavy bag is one of the oldest and most recognizable pieces of training equipment. It's used by boxers, mixed martial artists, self-defense practitioners, and fitness enthusiasts. Unfortunately, most people don't know how to use the heavy bag correctly. Heavy Bag Training teaches you everything you ever wanted to know about working out on the heavy bag. In this one-of-a-kind book, world-renowned self-defense expert Sammy Franco provides you with the knowledge, skills, and attitude necessary to maximize the training benefits of the bag. 8.5 x 5.5, paperback, photos, illus, 172 pages.

HEAVY BAG COMBINATIONS
The Ultimate Guide to Heavy Bag Punching Combinations
(Heavy Bag Training Series Book 2)
by Sammy Franco

Heavy Bag Combinations is the second book in Sammy Franco's best-selling Heavy Bag Training Series. This unique book is your ultimate guide to mastering devastating heavy bag punching combinations. With over 300+ photographs and detailed step-by-step instructions, Heavy Bag Combinations provides beginner, intermediate and advanced heavy bag workout combinations that will challenge you for the rest of your life! In fact, even the most experienced athlete will advance his fighting skills to the next level and beyond. 8.5 x 5.5, paperback, photos, illus, 248 pages.

HEAVY BAG WORKOUTS
A Hard-Core Guide to Heavy Bag Workout Routines
(Heavy Bag Training Series Book 3)
by Sammy Franco

Heavy Bag Workout is the third book in Sammy Franco's best-selling Heavy Bag Training Series. This unique book features over two dozen "out of the box" heavy bag workout routines that will maximize your fighting skills for boxing, mixed martial arts, kick boxing, self-defense, and personal fitness. 8.5 x 5.5, paperback, photos, illus, 208 pages.

HEAVY BAG BIBLE
3 Best-Selling Heavy Bag Books In One Massive Collection
(Heavy Bag Training Series Books 1, 2, 3)
by Sammy Franco

In this unprecedented book collection, world-renowned martial arts and self-defense expert, Sammy Franco takes his thirty years of teaching experience and gives you the most authoritative information for mastering the heavy bag. The Heavy Bag Bible includes Franco's three best-selling heavy bag books collected into one huge paperback collection. This massive 530+ page book contains the entire Heavy Bag Training Series, books 1-3. 8.5 x 5.5, paperback, photos, illus, 538 pages.

DOUBLE END BAG WORKOUT
For Boxing, Mixed Martial Arts & Self-Defense
by Sammy Franco

With over 200 detailed photographs, clear illustrations, and easy-to-follow instructions, Double End Bag Workout: For Boxing, Mixed Martial Arts and Self-Defense has everything you need to start training immediately. Double End Bag Workout also has beginner, intermediate and advanced workout routines that improve your speed, timing, accuracy, attack rhythm, and endurance. Whether you're an elite fighter or a complete beginner, this comprehensive book will take your boxing workout to the next level and beyond! 8.5 x 5.5, paperback, photos, illus, 260 pages.

THE COMPLETE BODY OPPONENT BAG BOOK
by Sammy Franco

In this one-of-a-kind book, Sammy Franco teaches you the many hidden training features of the body opponent bag that will improve your fighting skills and boost your conditioning. With detailed photographs, step-by-step instructions, and dozens of unique workout routines, The Complete Body Opponent Bag Book is the authoritative resource for mastering this lifelike punching bag. It covers stances, punching, kicking, grappling techniques, mobility and footwork, targets, fighting ranges, training gear, time based workouts, punching and kicking combinations, weapons training, grappling drills, ground fighting, and dozens of workouts. 8.5 x 5.5, paperback, 139 photos, illustrations, 206 pages.

KNOCKOUT
The Ultimate Guide to Sucker Punching
by Sammy Franco

Knockout is a one-of-a-kind book designed to teach you the lost art and science of sucker punching for real-world self-defense situations. With over 150 detailed photographs, 244 pages and dozens of easy-to-follow instructions, Knockout has everything you need to master the devastating art of sucker punching. Whether you are a beginner or advanced, student or teacher, Knockout teaches you brutally effective skills, battle-tested techniques, and proven strategies to get you home alive and in one piece. 8.5 x 5.5, paperback, 244 pages.

MAXIMUM DAMAGE
Hidden Secrets Behind Brutal Fighting Combinations
by Sammy Franco

Maximum Damage teaches you the quickest ways to beat your opponent in the street by exploiting his physical and psychological reactions in a fight. Learn how to stay two steps ahead of your adversary by knowing exactly how he will react to your strikes before they are delivered. In this unique book, reality based self-defense expert Sammy Franco reveals his unique Probable Reaction Dynamic (PRD) fighting method. Probable reaction dynamics are both a scientific and comprehensive offensive strategy based on the positional theory of combat. Regardless of your style of fighting, PRD training will help you overpower your opponent by seamlessly integrating your strikes into brutal fighting combinations that are fast, ferocious and final! 8.5 x 5.5, paperback, 240 photos, illustrations, 238 pages.

THE BIGGER THEY ARE, THE HARDER THEY FALL
How to Fight a Bigger and Stronger Opponent
by Sammy Franco

Sammy Franco was concerned that no book on the market successfully tackled the specific problem of fighting a larger, stronger opponent. In The Bigger They Are, The Harder They Fall, he addresses that all-important issue and delivers the solid information you'll need to win a street fight when the odds seem stacked against you. In this one-of-a-kind book, Sammy Franco prepares you both mentally and physically for the fight of your life. Unless you're a lineman for the NFL, there may come a day when you will face an opponent who can dominate you through sheer mass and power. Read and study this book before that day comes. 8.5 x 5.5, paperback, photos, illus, 212 pages.

CONTEMPORARY FIGHTING ARTS, LLC
"Real World Self-Defense Since 1989"
SammyFranco.com

www.ingramcontent.com/pod-product-compliance
Lightning Source LLC
Chambersburg PA
CBHW071512040426
42444CB00008B/1615